Letts

GCSE SUCCESS

VISUAL
REVISION
GUIDE

MATHEMATICS
INTERMEDIATE

Author
Fiona C Mapp

CONTENTS

NUMBER

ALGEBRA

SHAPE, SPACE AND MEASURES

HANDLING DATA

TYPES OF NUMBERS

NUMBER

SQUARE ROOTS AND CUBE ROOTS

$\sqrt{\ }$ is the square root sign. Taking the square root is the opposite of squaring. For example, $\sqrt{25} = \pm5$ since $5^2 = 25$, or $(-5)^2 = 25$.
$^3\sqrt{\ }$ is the cube root sign. Taking the cube root is the opposite of cubing. For example, $^3\sqrt{8} = 2$ since $2^3 = 8$.

SQUARES AND CUBES

SQUARE NUMBERS
Anything to the power 2 is square. For example, $6^2 = 6 \times 6 = 36$ (six squared).

Square numbers include:

1	4	9	16	25	36	49	64	81	100	. . .
(1 x 1)	(2 x 2)	(3 x 3)	(4 x 4)	(5 x 5)	(6 x 6)	(7 x 7)	(8 x 8)	(9 x 9)	(10 x 10)	

Square numbers can be illustrated by drawing squares:

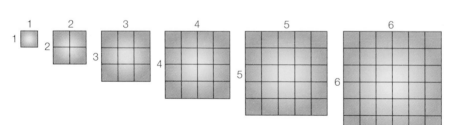

You need to know up to 15^2

CUBE NUMBERS
Anything to the power 3 is cube. For example, $5^3 = 5 \times 5 \times 5 = 125$ (five cubed).
Cube numbers include:

1	8	27	64	125	216 . . .
(1 x 1 x 1)	(2 x 2 x 2)	(3 x 3 x 3)	(4 x 4 x 4)	(5 x 5 x 5)	(6 x 6 x 6)

Cube numbers can be illustrated by drawing cubes:

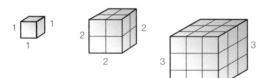
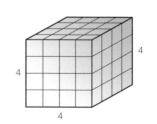

Examiner's Top Tip
It is important that you recognise square and cube numbers because they often appear in number sequences.

4

MULTIPLES

These are just the numbers in multiplication tables. For example, multiples of 8 are 8, 16, 24, 32, 40, . . .

RECIPROCALS

The reciprocal of a number $\frac{a}{x}$ is $\frac{x}{a}$ ($= x \div a$). Multiplying a number by its reciprocal always gives 1.

EXAMPLES

• The reciprocal of $\frac{2}{3}$ is $\frac{3}{2}$.
• The reciprocal of 4 is $\frac{1}{4}$ because 4 is the same as $\frac{4}{1}$.
• To find the reciprocal of $1\frac{2}{3}$, first put it in the form a/x (so $1\frac{2}{3} = \frac{5}{3}$), and then invert it ($\frac{3}{5}$).

FACTORS AND PRIMES

FACTORS

These are whole numbers which <u>divide</u> <u>exactly</u> into another number. For example, the factors of 20 are

1, 2, 4, 5, 10, 20.

Factors of 20 can be split up into factor pairs.

So
    1 x 20 = 20
    2 x 10 = 20
    4 x 5 = 20

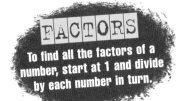

FACTORS
To find all the factors of a number, start at 1 and divide by each number in turn.

PRIME NUMBERS

These are numbers which have only two factors, <u>1 and itself</u>. Note that 1 is <u>not</u> a prime number. Prime numbers up to 20 are

2, 3, 5, 7, 11, 13, 17, 19.

PRIME FACTORS

These are factors which are prime. All numbers, except prime numbers, can be written as products of their prime factors.

EXAMPLE

The diagram below shows the prime factors of 360.
• Divide 360 by its first prime factor, 2.
• Divide 180 by its first prime factor, 2.
• Keep on going until the final number is prime.

<u>As a product of its prime factors 360 may be written as</u>:

$2 \times 2 \times 2 \times 3 \times 3 \times 5 = 360$
    or $2^3 \times 3^2 \times 5 = 360$

in <u>index</u> notation (using powers).

HIGHEST COMMON FACTOR (HCF)

The <u>largest factor</u> that two numbers have in common is called the <u>HCF</u>.

EXAMPLE

Find the HCF of 84 and 360.
• Write the numbers as products of their prime factors.
    $84 = 2 \times 2 \times 3 \times 7$
    $360 = 2 \times 2 \times 2 \times 3 \times 3 \times 5$
• Ring the factors in common
• These give the HCF $= 2 \times 2 \times 3 = 12$

LOWEST COMMON MULTIPLE (LCM)

This is the <u>lowest</u> number which is a <u>multiple</u> of two numbers.

EXAMPLE

Find the LCM of 6 and 8.
• Write the numbers as products of their prime factors.
• $8 = 2 \times 2 \times 2$
• $6 = 2 \times 3$
• 8 and 6 have a common prime factor of 2. So it is only counted once.
• The LCM of 6 and 8 is $2 \times 2 \times 2 \times 3 = 24$

QUICK TEST

1. List the prime numbers up to 20.

2. Find the HCF and LCM of 24 and 60.

3. Find a) $\sqrt{64}$ b) $^3\sqrt{216}$

4. Write down the reciprocals of a) $\frac{9}{12}$ b) $\frac{x}{p}$

— POSITIVE & NEGATIVE NUMBERS +

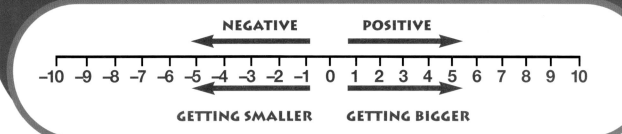

NEGATIVE ← _____ POSITIVE →

-10 -9 -8 -7 -6 -5 -4 -3 -2 -1 0 1 2 3 4 5 6 7 8 9 10

← GETTING SMALLER ___ GETTING BIGGER →

DIRECTED NUMBERS

These are numbers which may be <u>positive</u> or <u>negative</u>.
Positive are above zero, negative are below zero.

EXAMPLES
-10 is smaller than -8. $-10 < -8$
-4 is bigger than -8. $-4 > -8$
2 is bigger than -6. $2 > -6$

Directed numbers are often seen on the weather
forecast in winter. Quite often the temperature is below 0.
Aberdeen is the coldest at -8°C.
London is 6°C warmer than Manchester.

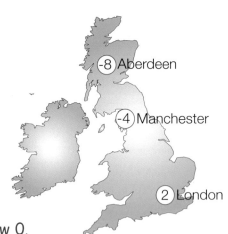

(-8) Aberdeen

(-4) Manchester

(2) London

INTEGERS

The integers are the set of numbers $\{\ldots, -3, -2, -1, 0, 1, 2, 3, \ldots\}$.
When referring to integers, the term <u>integral value</u> is used. A number
that is <u>non-integral</u> is not an integer.

MULTIPLYING AND DIVIDING DIRECTED NUMBERS

<u>Multiply</u> <u>and</u> <u>divide</u> <u>the</u> <u>numbers</u> <u>as</u> <u>normal.</u>
<u>Then</u> <u>find</u> <u>the</u> <u>sign</u> <u>for</u> <u>the</u> <u>answer</u> <u>using</u> <u>these</u> <u>rules:</u>

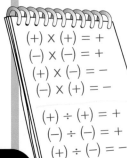

$(+) \times (+) = +$
$(-) \times (-) = +$
$(+) \times (-) = -$
$(-) \times (+) = -$

$(+) \div (+) = +$
$(-) \div (-) = +$
$(+) \div (-) = -$
$(-) \div (+) = -$

- two <u>like</u> signs (both + or both –) give positive,
- two <u>unlike</u> signs (one + and the other –)
  give negative.

EXAMPLES
$-6 \times (+4) = -24$ $-12 \div (-3) = 4$
$-6 \times (-3) = 18$ $20 \div (-4) = -5$

Examiner's Top Tip
The rules of multiplication/
division need to be
remembered. You could
quite easily use these laws
when multiplying out
brackets in algebra.

6

ADDING AND SUBTRACTING DIRECTED NUMBERS

EXAMPLE
The temperature at 6 a.m. was –5°C. By 10 a.m. it had risen 8 degrees. So the new temperature was 3°C.

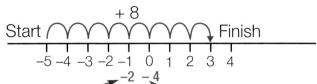

EXAMPLE
Find the value of –2 – 4.

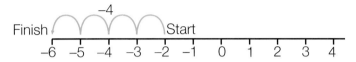

This represents the
<u>sign</u> of the number.
Start at –2.

This represents the operation
of <u>subtraction</u>. Move 4 places
to the left.

So –2 – 4 = –6
When the number to be added (or subtracted) is <u>negative</u>, the normal direction of movement is <u>reversed</u>.

EXAMPLE   –4 – (–3) is the same as –4 + 3 = –1

The negative changes the <u>direction</u>.   **Move 3 places to the <u>right</u>.**

When two (+) or two (–) signs are together, these rules are used:

+(+) → +
–(–) → + } <u>like</u> signs give a <u>positive</u>,

+(–) → –
–(+) → – } <u>unlike</u> signs give a <u>negative</u>.

EXAMPLES
–6 + (–2) = –6 – 2 = –8   –2 – (+6) = –2 – 6 = –8
4 – (–3) = 4 + 3 = 7   9 + (–3) = 9 – 3 = 6

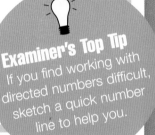

Examiner's Top Tip
If you find working with
directed numbers difficult,
sketch a quick number
line to help you.

NEGATIVE NUMBERS ON THE CALCULATOR

The +/– or (–) key on the calculator gives a
<u>negative</u> number.
For example, to get –6, press 6   +/– or
(–)   6 .
This represents the <u>sign</u>.

EXAMPLE
–4 – (–2) = –2
is keyed in the calculator like this:

4   +/–   –   2   +/–   =

          ↑   ↑   ↑
        sign   operation   sign

Make sure you know how to enter negative
numbers in <u>your</u> calculator.

* * *

QUICK TEST

1. If the temperature was –12°C at 2 a.m., and it rose by 15 degrees by 11 a.m., what was the
   temperature at 11 a.m.?

2. Work these out, without a calculator.

   a) –2 – (–6)   b) –9 + (–7)   c) –2 x 6

   d) –9 + (–3)   e) –20 ÷ (–4)   f) –18 ÷ (–3)

   g) 4 – (–3)   h) –7 + (–3)   i) –9 x –4

1. 3°C   2. a) 4 b) –16 c) –12 d) –12 e) 5 f) 6 g) 7 h) –10 i) 36

EQUIVALENT FRACTIONS

These are fractions which have the same value.

EXAMPLE

 $\frac{1}{2}$ $\frac{2}{4}$ $\frac{3}{6}$ $\frac{4}{8}$

From the diagrams it can be seen that $\frac{1}{2} = \frac{2}{4} = \frac{3}{6} = \frac{4}{8}$. They are equivalent fractions. Fractions can be changed to their equivalent by multiplying or dividing both the numerator and denominator by the same amount.

EXAMPLES

Change $\frac{5}{7}$ to its equivalent fraction with a denominator of 28.

Multiply top and bottom by 4.
So $\frac{20}{28}$ is equivalent to $\frac{5}{7}$.

Change $\frac{40}{60}$ to its equivalent fraction with a denominator of 3.

Divide top and bottom by 20.
So $\frac{40}{60}$ is equivalent to $\frac{2}{3}$.

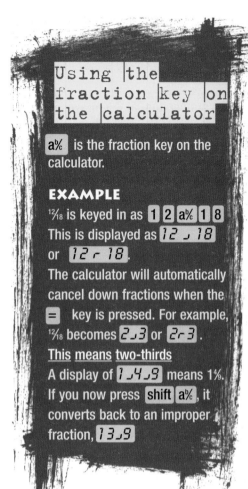

Using the fraction key on the calculator

a% is the fraction key on the calculator.

EXAMPLE

$\frac{12}{18}$ is keyed in as 1 2 a% 1 8
This is displayed as 12⌐18
or 12⌐18.
The calculator will automatically cancel down fractions when the = key is pressed. For example, $\frac{12}{18}$ becomes 2⌐3 or 2⌐3. This means two-thirds
A display of 1⌐4⌐9 means 1$\frac{4}{9}$. If you now press shift a%, it converts back to an improper fraction, 13⌐9

MULTIPLICATION AND DIVISION OF FRACTIONS

When multiplying and dividing fractions, write out whole or mixed numbers as improper fractions before starting.

EXAMPLE

$\frac{2}{9} \times \frac{4}{7} = \frac{2 \times 4}{9 \times 7} = \frac{8}{63}$ ◄── Multiply numerators together.
◄── Multiply denominators together.

Change a division into a multiplication by turning the second fraction upside down and multiplying both fractions together; that is, multiply by the reciprocal.

EXAMPLE

$\frac{7}{9} \div \frac{12}{18} = \frac{7}{9} \times \frac{18}{12}$

$= \frac{126}{108} = 1\frac{1}{6}$

Take the reciprocal of the second fraction.

Rewrite the answer as a mixed number.

PROPORTIONAL CHANGES WITH FRACTIONS AND PERCENTAGES

INCREASE AND DECREASE
There are two methods. Use the one that is familiar to you.

EXAMPLE
Last year there were 290 people belonging to a gym. This year there are $\frac{3}{5}$ more. How many people now belong?

Remember 'of' means multiply

METHOD 1
$\frac{3}{5} \times 290 = 174$
$290 + 174 = 464$ people

Work out $\frac{3}{5}$ of 290. Add this on to the original number.

METHOD 2
Increasing by $\frac{3}{5}$ is the same as multiplying by $1\frac{3}{5}$ $(1 + \frac{3}{5})$.
$1\frac{3}{5} \times 290 = 464$
On the calculator key in 1 a% 3 a% 5 x 290 =

Use the fraction key to work this out, if possible. If this question is on the non-calculator paper, remember to:
• Divide 290 by the denominator $290 \div 5 = 58$ • Multiply by the numerator $58 \times 3 = 174$
• Now add onto the original value

ADDITION AND SUBTRACTION OF FRACTIONS

These examples show the basic principles of adding and subtracting fractions.

EXAMPLE

$\frac{1}{8} + \frac{3}{4}$

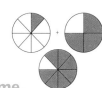

- First make the denominators the same: $\frac{3}{4} = \frac{6}{8}$

$\frac{3}{4}$ is **equivalent** to $\frac{6}{8}$.

$= \frac{1}{8} + \frac{6}{8}$

- Replace $\frac{3}{4}$ with $\frac{6}{8}$ so that the denominators are the same.

$= \frac{7}{8}$

- Add the numerators $1 + 6 = 7$. **Do** **not** **add** the denominators; the denominator stays the same number.

EXAMPLE

$\frac{9}{12} - \frac{1}{3}$

- First make the denominators the same: $\frac{1}{3} = \frac{4}{12}$
  $\frac{1}{3}$ is equivalent to $\frac{4}{12}$.

$= \frac{9}{12} - \frac{4}{12}$

- Replace the $\frac{1}{3}$ with $\frac{4}{12}$.

$= \frac{5}{12}$

- Subtract the numerators but **not** the denominators; the denominator stays the same number.

On a calculator you would type in:

| 9 | a⅙ | 12 | – | 1 | a⅙ | 3 | = |

FRACTIONS

A fraction is a part of a whole one. $\frac{4}{5}$ means 4 parts out of 5.
The top number is the numerator. The bottom one is the denominator.
A fraction like $\frac{4}{5}$ is called a proper fraction.
A fraction like $\frac{24}{17}$ is called an improper fraction.
$2\frac{1}{2}$ is called a mixed number.

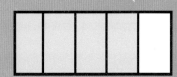

QUICK TEST

1. Without using a calculator work out the following:

   a) $\frac{2}{9} + \frac{3}{27}$ b) $\frac{3}{5} - \frac{1}{4}$

   c) $\frac{6}{9} \times \frac{72}{104}$ d) $\frac{8}{9} \div \frac{2}{3}$

   e) $\frac{4}{7} - \frac{1}{3}$ f) $\frac{2}{7} \div 1\frac{1}{2}$

   g) $\frac{7}{11} \div \frac{22}{14}$ h) $\frac{2}{9} + \frac{4}{7}$

2. Calculate $\frac{2}{9}$ of £180.

3. $\frac{7}{12}$ more rain fell this year. If 156 mm fell last year, how much fell this year?

1. a) $\frac{1}{3}$ b) $\frac{7}{20}$ c) $\frac{6}{13}$ d) $1\frac{1}{3}$ e) $\frac{5}{21}$ f) $\frac{4}{21}$ g) $\frac{49}{121}$ h) $\frac{50}{63}$ 2. £40   3. 247 mm

DECIMALS

DECIMAL PLACES (D.P.)

<u>When rounding numbers to a specified number of decimal places</u>:
- look at the last number that is wanted (if rounding 12.367 to 2 d.p., look at the 6 which is the second d.p.);
- look at the number to the right of it (look at the number which is not needed – the 7);
- if it is <u>5 or more</u>, then <u>round up the last digit</u> (7 is greater than 5, so round up the 6 to a 7);
- if it is <u>less than 5</u>, then the digit remains the <u>same</u>

EXAMPLES

Round 12.49 to 1 d.p.
12.4<u>9</u> rounds up to 12.5.

```
                              12.49
                                ↓
          ├──┬──┬──┬──┬──┬──┬──┤
          12.4   12.45    12.5
```

Round 8.735 to 2 d.p.
8.73<u>5</u> rounds up to 8.74.

```
                    8.735
                      ↓
          ├──┬──┬──┬──┬──┬──┬──┤
         8.73   8.735    8.74
```

Round 9.624 to 2 d.p.
9.62<u>4</u> rounds to 9.62

```
                 9.624
                   ↓
          ├──┬──┬──┬──┬──┬──┬──┤
         9.62   9.625    9.63
```

ORDERING DECIMALS

<u>When ordering decimals</u>:
- first write them with the same number of figures after the decimal point;
- then compare whole numbers, digits in the tenths place, digits in the hundredths place, and so on.

EXAMPLES

Arrange these numbers in order of size, smallest first:
6.21, 6.023, 6.4, 6.04, 2.71, 9.4
First rewrite them:
6.210, 6.023, 6.400, 6.040, 2.710, 9.400
Then re-order them:
2.710, 6.023, 6.040, 6.210, 6.400, 9.400

> Remember, hundredths are smaller than tenths
> $\frac{10}{100} = \frac{1}{10}$ so $\frac{6}{100} < \frac{1}{10}$

CALCULATIONS WITH DECIMALS

When adding and subtracting decimals, the decimal points need to go under each other.

EXAMPLES

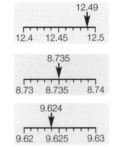

```
  27.46 ↙
  7.291 +
  34.751
   1  1
```
- Line up the digits carefully
- Put the decimal points under each other

```
  6 9 1
  1 7̶.0̶0̶
  12.84 –
   4.16
```
- The decimal point in the answer will be in line

When <u>multiplying</u> decimals, the answer must have the same number of decimal places as the total number of decimal places in the numbers which are being multiplied.

EXAMPLES

```
  24.6
    7 x
  172.2
   3 4
```
- Remember to check with your calculator

Multiply 246 by 7 = 1722, ignoring the decimal point. 24.6 has 1 number after the decimal point. The answer must have 1 decimal place (1 d.p.).

So 24.6 x 7 = 172.2

Work out 4.52 x 0.2

```
  452
    2 x
  904
   1
```

Work out 452 x 2, ignoring the decimal points.
4.52 has 2 d.p. 0.2 has 1 d.p.
So the answer must have 3 d.p.

904 ➡ 0.904 Move the decimal point 3 places.

So 4.52 x 0.2 = 0.904

When <u>dividing</u> decimals, divide as normal, placing the decimal points in line.

EXAMPLE

```
     4.8
  3 ) 14.4
        1 2
```

> Put the decimal points in line.

A decimal point is used to separate whole number columns from fractional columns.

EXAMPLE

Thousands	Hundreds	Tens	Units	.	Tenths	Hundredths	Thousandths
5	9	2	4	.	1	6	3

Decimal Point

• The 1 means $\frac{1}{10}$. • The 6 means $\frac{6}{100}$. • The 3 means $\frac{3}{1000}$.

RECURRING DECIMALS
A decimal that recurs is shown by placing a dot over the numbers that repeat.

EXAMPLES

$0.333\ldots = 0.\dot{3}$ $0.17777\ldots = 0.1\dot{7}$ $0.232323\ldots = 0.\dot{2}\dot{3}$

MULTIPLYING AND DIVIDING BY NUMBERS BETWEEN 0 AND 1

When _multiplying_ by numbers between 0 and 1, the result is _smaller_ than the starting value.
When _dividing_ by numbers between 0 and 1, the result is _bigger_ than the starting value.

EXAMPLES

$6 \times 0.1 = 0.6$ $6 \div 0.1 = 60$
$6 \times 0.01 = 0.06$ $6 \div 0.01 = 600$
$6 \times 0.001 = 0.006$ $6 \div 0.001 = 6000$

The result is smaller than the starting value.   The result is bigger than the starting value.

QUICK TEST

1. Without using a calculator work out the following:

a) 27.16 + 9.32   b) 29.04 – 11.361   c) 12.8 x 2.1

d) 49.2 ÷ 4   e) 600 x 0.01   f) 520 x 0.1

g) 20 x 0.02   h) 37 x 0.0001   i) 400 ÷ 0.1

j) 450 ÷ 0.01   k) 470 ÷ 0.001   l) 650 ÷ 0.02

2. Round the following numbers to 2 decimal places:

a) 7.469
b) 12.0372
c) 9.365
d) 10.042
e) 8.1794

Examiner's Top Tip
Multiplying and dividing by numbers between 0 and 1 usually occur on the non-calculator paper – it is wise to practise these by writing out several calculations and then checking the answer with a calculator.

1. a) 36.48 b) 17.679 c) 26.88 d) 12.3 e) 6 f) 52 g) 0.4 h) 0.0037 i) 4000 j) 45000 k) 470000 l) 32500
2. a) 7.47 b) 12.04 c) 9.37 d) 10.04 e) 8.18

11

PERCENTAGE OF A QUANTITY

The word '**of**' means **multiply**. For example, 40% of £600 becomes $\frac{40}{100}$ x 600 = £240

On the calculator key in

40 ÷ 100 x 600 =

If this is on the non-calculator paper

• Work out 10% first by dividing by 10
  e.g. **600 ÷10 = £60.**
• Multiply by 4 to get 40% i.e. 4 x 60 = £240.

Examiner's Top Tip
Percentage questions appear frequently at GCSE. If there is a percentage question on the non-calculator paper, try and work out what 10% is equal to, as shown in the examples above.

This is just like a percentage of a quantity question.

EXAMPLE
A meal for four costs £92.20. VAT is charged at 17.5%.

• VAT is a tax which is added on to the cost of most items.

a) How much VAT is there to pay on the meal?

b) What is the final price of the meal?

a) 17.5% of £92.20
= $\frac{17.5}{100}$ x 92.20 = £16.14
(to the nearest penny)
VAT = £16.14

Value added tax (VAT)

b) Price of meal = £92.20 + £16.14 = £108.34

An alternative is to use a scale factor method.

• an increase of 17.5%, is the same as multiplying by 1 + $\frac{17.5}{100}$ = 1.175.

£92.20 x 1.175 = £108.34 (to the nearest penny).

PERCENTAGES ①

THESE ARE FRACTIONS WITH A DENOMINATOR OF 100

% IS THE <u>PERCENTAGE</u> SIGN.

75% MEANS $\frac{75}{100}$ (THIS IS ALSO EQUAL TO $\frac{3}{4}$).

75%

PERCENTAGE INCREASE AND DECREASE

The answer will be a percentage so multiply by 100%.

% change = $\frac{change}{original}$ x 100%

EXAMPLE
A coat costs £125. In a sale it is reduced to £85.
What is the percentage reduction?
Reduction = £125 – £85 = £40
$\frac{40}{125}$ x 100% = 32%

£125 £85

EXAMPLE
Matthew bought a flat for £45000. Three years later, he sold it for £62000.
What was his percentage profit?
Profit   = £62000 – £45000
         = £17000
% Profit = $\frac{17000}{45000}$ x 100% = 37.78%

ONE QUANTITY AS A PERCENTAGE OF ANOTHER

To make the answer a <u>percentage</u>, multiply by <u>100%</u>.

EXAMPLE
In a carton of milk, 6.2 g of the contents are fat.
If 2.5 g of the fat is saturated, what percentage is this?
$\frac{2.5}{6.2} \times 100\% = 40.3\%$ (to 1 d.p.)
On the calculator key in
2.5 ÷ 6.2 × 100 =

Multiply by 100% to get a percentage.

$$Fraction \xrightarrow{\times 100\%} Percentage$$

REVERSE PERCENTAGE PROBLEMS

Reverse percentage is when the <u>original</u> <u>quantity</u> is calculated.
EXAMPLE
The price of a television is reduced by 20% in the sales.
It <u>now</u> costs £250. What was the original price?

- The sale price is 100% − 20% = 80% of the pre-sale price.
    $\frac{80}{100} = 0.8$
    0.8 × (price) = £250
    price = 250/0.8 = £312.50

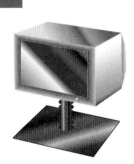

$$original\ price \underset{\div\ 0.8}{\overset{\times\ 0.8}{\rightleftarrows}} new\ price$$

80%
It is 80% of the original price which is being found, not 80% of the new one.

- Always check the answer is sensible.
- Is the original price more than the sale price?

QUICK TEST

1. Work out 30% of £700.

2. Sarah got 94 out of 126 in a Maths test. What percentage did she get?

3. Reece weighed 6 lb when he was born. If his weight has increased by 65%, how much does he now weigh?

4. The price of a hi-fi is reduced by 15% in the sales. It now costs £350. What was the original price?

5.
Super's football boots	Joe's football boots
$\frac{1}{3}$ off	28% off

If a pair of football boots costs £49.99, which shop sells them cheaper in the sale and what is the price?

REPEATED PERCENTAGE CHANGE

EXAMPLE
A car was bought for £8000 in 1994. Each year it depreciated in value by 20%. What was the car worth 3 years later?

Work these questions out year by year.

METHOD 1

- Find 80% of the value of the car first.
  Year 1 $\frac{80}{100}$ x £8000 = £6400
- Then work out the value year by year.
  Year 2 $\frac{80}{100}$ x £6400 = £5120 (£6400 depreciates in value by 20%.)
  Year 3 $\frac{80}{100}$ x £5120 = £4096 after 3 years (£5120 depreciates by 20%.)

Beware: do not do 3 x 20 = 60% reduction over 3 years!

METHOD 2

- A quick way to work this out uses the scale factor method.
- Finding 80% of the value of the car is the same as multiplying by 0.8. 0.8 is the scale factor.
  Year 1   0.8 x £8000 = £6400
  Year 2   0.8 x £6400 = £5120
  Year 3   0.8 x £5120 = £4096

This is the same as working out $(0.8)^3$ x 8000 = £4096
A much quicker way if you understand it!

SIMPLE INTEREST

This is the interest that is sometimes paid on money in banks and building societies. The interest is paid each year (per annum or p.a.) and is the same amount each year.

EXAMPLE
Jonathan has £2500 in his savings account. Simple interest is paid at 4.4% p.a. How much does he have in his account at the end of the year?

This is a 'percentage of' question

100 + 4.4 = 104.4% (increasing by 4.4 % is the same as multiplying by 100 + 44 = 104.4 %)
Total savings = $\frac{104.4}{100}$ x £2500 = £2610
Interest paid = £2610 − £2500 = £110

Note: If the money was in the account for 4 years, the interest at the end of the 4 years would be 4 x £110 = £440

COMPOUND INTEREST

This is the type of interest where the bank pays interest on the interest earned as well as on the original money.

EXAMPLE
If Jonathan has £2500 in his savings account and compound interest is paid at 4.4% p.a., how much will he have in his account after 4 years?

METHOD 1
Year 1: $\frac{104.4}{100}$ x £2500 = £2610
Year 2: 1.044 x £2610 = £2724.84
Year 3: 1.044 x £2724.84 = £2844.73
Year 4: 1.044 x £2844.73 = £2969.90
Total = £2969.90 (nearest penny)

METHOD 2
$\frac{104.4}{100}$ = 1.044 is the multiplicative factor
£2500 x 1.044 x 1.044 x 1.044 x 1.044
= 2500 x $(1.044)^4$
Total = £2969.90 (nearest penny)

Method 2 uses the scale factor method

TAX AND NATIONAL INSURANCE

NATIONAL INSURANCE
National Insurance (NI) is usually deducted as a percentage from a wage.

EXAMPLE
Sue earns £1402.65 a month. National Insurance at 9% is deducted. How much NI must she pay?
9% of £1402.65 = 0.09 x £1402.65 = £126.24

INCOME TAX
A percentage of a wage or salary is removed as income tax.
Personal allowances must first be removed in order to obtain the taxable income.

EXAMPLE
Harold earns £190 per week. His first £62 is not taxable but the remainder is taxed at 24%.
How much income tax does he pay each week?
Taxable income = £190 – £62 = £128
24% tax = 0.24 x £128 = £30.72
Tax per week = £30.72

Examiner's Top Tip
Being able to answer questions like the examples shown in this section is important – not only because they appear on the examination paper but because you will come across them in everyday life. Most of the examples are 'percentage of' questions.

PERCENTAGES 2

There are really only 2 types of percentage questions:

1. 'Percentage of'
Here you are given the percentage so you ÷ 100

2. Writing your answer as a percentage
Here you need to work out a percentage so you X 100

QUICK TEST

1. Charlotte has £4250 in the bank. If the interest rate is 6.8% p.a., how much interest on her savings will she get at the end of the year?

2. A car costs £6000 cash or can be bought by hire purchase with a 30% deposit followed by 12 monthly instalments of £365. Find:
   a) the deposit
   b) the total amount paid for the car on hire purchase

3. A flat was bought in 1998 for £62000. In 1999 the price increased by 20% and then by a further 35% in 2000. How much was the flat worth at the end of 2000?

4. Fiona has £3200 savings. If compound interest is paid at 3% p.a., how much will she have in her account after three years?

1. £289 2 a) £1800 b) £6180 3. £100440 4. £3496.73

15

EQUIVALENCES BETWEEN FRACTIONS, DECIMALS AND PERCENTAGES

FRACTIONS TO DECIMALS TO PERCENTAGES

Fractions, decimals and percentages all mean the same thing but are just written in a different way.

Fraction	Decimal	Percentage
$\frac{1}{2}$	0.5	50%
$\frac{1}{3}$	0.3̇3̇	33.3̇%
$\frac{2}{3}$	0.6̇6̇	66.6̇%
$\frac{1}{4}$	0.25	25%
$\frac{3}{4}$	0.75	75%
$\frac{1}{5}$	0.2	20%
$\frac{1}{8}$	0.125	12.5%
$\frac{3}{8}$	0.375	37.5%
$\frac{1}{10}$	0.1	10%
$\frac{1}{100}$	0.01	1%

$3 \div 4$ → $\times 100\%$ →

The above table shows
• Some common fractions and their equivalents which you need to learn.
• How to convert fractions ⟶ decimals ⟶ percentages.

ORDERING DIFFERENT NUMBERS

When putting fractions, decimals and percentages in order of size, it is best to change them all to decimals first.

EXAMPLE

$\frac{3}{5}$, 0.65, 0.273, 27%, 62%, $\frac{4}{9}$ ⟵ Place in order of size, smallest first

0.6, 0.65, 0.273, 0.27, 0.62, 0.4̇4̇ ⟵ Put into decimals first

0.27, 0.273, 0.4̇4̇, 0.6, 0.62, 0.65 ⟵ Now order

Examiner's Top Tip
Get a friend to test you on the equivalences between fractions, decimals and percentages as you need to learn them.

QUICK TEST

1. Change the following fractions into a) decimals b) percentages

   i) $\frac{2}{7}$ ii) $\frac{3}{5}$ iii) $\frac{8}{9}$

2. Place in order of size, smallest first:

   $\frac{2}{5}$, 0.42, 0.041, $\frac{1}{3}$, 5%, 26%

1. i)a) 0.2857 b) 28.57% (2 d.p.) ii)a) 0.6 b) 60% iii)a) 0.88 b) 88.88% 2. 0.041, 5%, 26%, $\frac{1}{3}$, $\frac{2}{5}$, 0.42

USING A CALCULATOR

IMPORTANT CALCULATOR KEYS

This calculator is an imaginary one to show you some of the most important keys. Make sure you are familiar with your own calculator.

Practise using your own calculator. Make sure you know where these keys are

Shift or 2nd or Inv allow 2nd functions to be carried out.

allows a fraction to be put in the calculator

– or +/- changes positive numbers to negative ones

bracket keys

often puts the x10 part in when working in standard form.

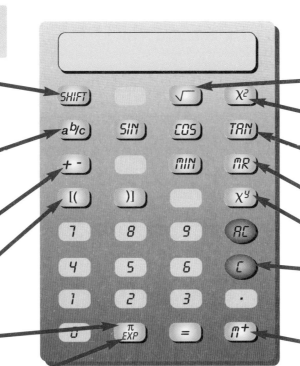

square root

square button

trigonometric buttons

memory keys

works out powers

cancels only the last key you have pressed

all memory keys

pressing shift EXP often gives π

EXAMPLE

$$\frac{15 \times 10 + 46}{9.3 \times 2.1} = 10.04 \text{ (2 d.p.)}$$

This may be keyed in as:
[(... 15 x 10 + 46 ...)] ÷ [(... 9.3 x 2.1 ...)] =

The above could be as easily done using the memory keys. Try writing down the key sequence for yourself.

CALCULATING POWERS

 or is used for calculating powers such as 2^7.

- Use the power key on the calculator to work out 2^7.
- Write down calculator keys used.
- Check that you obtain the answer 128.

Now try writing down the keys that would be needed for these calculations. Check that you get the right answers.

a) $\dfrac{2.9 \times 3.6}{(4.2 + 3.7)} = 1.322$ b) $9^{\frac{1}{3}} \times 4^5 = 2130$ c) $\dfrac{3 \times (5.2)^2}{9.6 \times (12.4)^3} = 4.432 \times 10^{-3}$

QUICK TEST

Work these out on your calculator:

a) $\dfrac{27.1 \times 6.4}{9.3 + 2.7}$ b) $\dfrac{(9.3)^4}{2.7 \times 3.6}$

c) $\sqrt{\dfrac{25^2}{4\pi}}$ d) $\dfrac{5}{9}(25 - 10)$

Examiner's Top Tip
Make sure you know how to use the power key as it saves lots of time.

a) 14.45 (2 d.p.)   b) 769.6 (1 d.p.)   c) 7.052 (3 d.p.)   d) $8\frac{1}{3}$ or 8.3

SIGNIFICANT FIGURES (S.F. OR SIG. FIG.)

Apply the same rule as with decimal places: if the next digit is 5 or more, round up. The 1st significant figure is the first digit which is not zero. The 2nd, 3rd, 4th,…. significant figures follow on after the 1st digit. They may or may not be zeros.

EXAMPLES

6.4027 has 5 s.f. — 1st 2nd 3rd 4th 5th

0.0004701 has 4 s.f. — 1st 2nd 3rd 4th

> Take care when rounding that you do not change the place values.

EXAMPLES

Number	to 3 s.f.	to 2 s.f.	to 1 s.f.
4.207	4.21	4.2	4
4379	4380	4400	4000
0.006209	0.00621	0.0062	0.006

After rounding the last digit, you must fill in the end zeros.
For example, 4380 = 4400 to 2 s.f. (not 44).

ESTIMATES AND APPROXIMATIONS

Estimating is a good way of checking answers.
• Round the numbers to 'easy' numbers, usually 1 or 2 significant figures.
• Work out the estimate using these easy numbers.
• Use the symbol ≈, which means 'approximately equal to'.
For multiplying or dividing, never approximate a number with zero.
Use 0.1, 0.01, 0.001, etc.

EXAMPLES
a) 8.93 x 25.09 ≈ 10 x 25 = 250
b) $(6.29)^2 \approx 6^2 = 36$
c) $\frac{296 \times 52.1}{9.72 \times 1.14} \approx \frac{300 \times 50}{10 \times 1} = \frac{15000}{10} = 1500$
d) 0.096 x 79.2 ≈ 0.1 x 80 = 8

EXAMPLE
Jack does the calculation $\frac{9.6 \times 103}{(2.9)^2}$

a) Estimate the answer to this calculation, without using a calculator.
b) Jack's answer is 1175.7. Is this the right order of magnitude?

a) Estimate $\frac{9.6 \times 103}{(2.9)^2} \approx \frac{10 \times 100}{3^2} = \frac{1000}{9} \approx \frac{1000}{10} = 100$

> Right order of magnitude means 'about the right size'

b) Jack's answer is not the right order of magnitude. It is 10 times too big.

When adding and subtracting, very small numbers may be approximated to zero.

EXAMPLES
109.6 + 0.0002 ≈ 110 + 0 = 110   63.87 − 0.01 ≈ 64 − 0 = 64

> **Examiner's Top Tip**
> Questions which involve approximating are common on the non-calculator paper. For most of these questions, you are expected to round to 1 significant figure. Even if you find the calculation difficult, show your approximations to help pick up method marks.

CHECKING CALCULATIONS

When checking calculations, the process can be reversed like this.

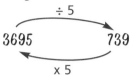

$$3695 \xrightarrow{\div 5} 739$$
$$3695 \xleftarrow{\times 5} 739$$

EXAMPLE

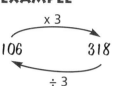

$$106 \xrightarrow{\times 3} 318$$
$$106 \xleftarrow{\div 3} 318$$

$106 \times 3 = 318$
Check: $318 \div 3 = 106$

APPROXIMATING & CHECKING CALCULATIONS

CALCULATIONS

When solving problems the answers should be rounded sensibly.

Round to 2 d.p. because the values in the question are to 2 d.p.

EXAMPLE
$95.26 \times 6.39 = 608.7114 = 608.71$ (2 d.p.)

EXAMPLE
Jackie has £9.37. She divides it equally between 5 people. How much does each person receive?
$£9.37 \div 5 = £1.874$
$\qquad\qquad = £1.87$

Round to 1.87 as it is money

EXAMPLE
Paint is sold in 8 litre tins. Sandra needs 27 litres of paint. How many tins must she buy?
$27 \div 8 = 3$ remainder 3
Sandra needs 4 tins of paint.
Sandra would not have enough paint with 3 tins, since she is 3 litres short. Hence the number of tins of paint must be rounded up.

When rounding remainders, consider the context of the question.

You will lose marks if you do not write money to 2 d.p. If the answer to a money calculation is £9.7, __always__ write it to 2 d.p. as £9.70.

QUICK TEST

1. Round the following numbers to 3 significant figures (3 s.f.):

   a) 0.003786   b) 27490   c) 307250

2. Estimate the answer to $\dfrac{(29.4)^2 + 106}{2.2 \times 5.1}$

3. Sukvinder decided to decorate her living room. The total area of the walls was 48 m². If one roll of wallpaper covers 5 m² of wall, how many rolls of wallpaper did Sukvinder need?

4. Thomas earned £109.25 for working a 23-hour week. How much was he paid per hour? Check your calculation by estimating.

1. a) 0.00379 b) 27500 c) 307000 2. 100 3. 10 rolls of wallpaper 4. £4.75

SHARING A QUANTITY IN A GIVEN RATIO

- Add up the total parts.
- Work out what one part is worth.
- Work out what the other parts are worth.

EXAMPLE

£20 000 is shared in the ratio 1 : 4 between Ewan and Leroy.
How much does each receive?

1 + 4 = 5 parts

5 parts = £20 000

1 part = $\frac{£20\ 000}{5}$ = £4000

So Ewan gets 1 x £4000 = £4000 and Leroy gets 4 x £4000 = £16 000.

INCREASING AND DECREASING IN A GIVEN RATIO

9 cm

3 3 3

- *Divide to get one part.*
- *Multiply for each new part.*

EXAMPLE

A photograph of length 9 cm is to be enlarged in the ratio 5 : 3.
What is the length of the enlarged photograph?
- *Divide 9 cm by 3 to get 1 part.*
  9 ÷ 3 = 3
- *Multiply this by 5. So 5 x 3 = 15 cm on the enlarged photograph.*

15 cm

3 3 3 3 3

EXAMPLE

A house took 8 people 6 days to build.
At the same rate how long would it take 3 people?
Time for 8 people = 6 days.
Time for 1 person = 8 x 6 = 48 days.
It takes 1 person longer to build the house.
Time for 3 people = $\frac{48}{3}$ = 16 days.
3 people will take $\frac{1}{3}$ of the time taken by 1 person.

EXAMPLE

A recipe for 4 people needs 1600 g of flour.
How much is needed for 6 people?
- *Divide 1600 g by 4, so 400 g for 1 person.*
- *Multiply by 6, so 6 x 400 g = 2400 g for 6 people.*

FLOUR

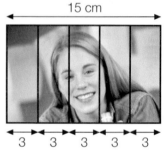

Examiner's Top Tip
When answering problems of the type shown here always try and work out what a unit (or one) is worth. You should then be able to work out what any other value is worth.

BEST BUYS

Use unit amounts to decide which is the better value for money.

EXAMPLE

The same brand of coffee is sold in two different sized jars.
Which jar represents the better value for money?

- Find the cost per gram for both jars.
  100 g costs 186p so 186 ÷ 100 = 1.86p per gram.
  250 g costs 247p so 247 ÷ 250 = 0.988p per gram.
- Since the larger jar costs less per gram it is the better value for money.

RATIOS

- **A ratio is used to compare two or more related quantities.**
- **'Compared to' is replaced with two dots : For example, '16 boys compared to 20 girls' can be written as 16 : 20.**
- **To simplify ratios, divide both parts of the ratio by the highest factor. For example, 16 : 20 = 4 : 5 (Divide both sides by 4).**

EXAMPLES
- **Simplify the ratio 21 : 28.**
  21 : 28 = 3 : 4 (Divide both sides by 7).
- **The ratio of red flowers to yellow flowers can be written:**
  10 : 4
  $= \frac{10}{2} : \frac{4}{2}$
  = 5 : 2

In other words, for every 5 red flowers there are 2 yellow flowers.
To express the ratio 5 : 2 in the ratio n : 1, divide both sides by 2.
$= \frac{5}{2} : 2$
= 2.5 : 1

QUICK TEST

1. Write the following ratios in their simplest form:

   a) 12 : 15

   b) 6 : 12

   c) 25 : 10

2. Three sisters share 60 sweets between them in the ratios 2 : 3 : 7. How many sweets does each sister receive?

3. If 15 oranges cost £1.80, how much will 23 identical oranges cost?

4. A map is being enlarged in the ratio 12 : 7. If the road length was 21 cm on the original map, what is the length of the road on the enlarged map?

$$x^a \times x^b = x^{a+b}$$

INDICES

An index is sometimes known as a power.

EXAMPLES

6^4 is read as 6 to the <u>power</u> <u>of 4</u>. It means 6 x 6 x 6 x 6.

2^7 is read as 2 to the <u>power</u> <u>7</u>. It means 2 x 2 x 2 x 2 x 2 x 2 x 2.

the <u>base</u> ➞ a^b ⬅ the <u>index</u> or <u>power</u>

The <u>base</u> has to be the <u>same</u> when the rules of indices are applied.

RULES OF INDICES

Indices are a very common topic on the non-calculator paper.

<u>You</u> <u>need</u> <u>to</u> <u>learn</u> <u>these</u> <u>rules</u>:

- When <u>multiplying</u>, <u>add</u> the powers.
  $4^7 \times 4^3 = 4^{7+3} = 4^{10}$

- When <u>dividing</u>, <u>subtract</u> the powers.
  $6^9 \div 6^4 = 6^{9-4} = 6^5$

- When <u>raising</u> <u>one</u> <u>power</u> <u>to</u> <u>another</u>, <u>multiply</u> the powers.
  $(7^2)^4 = 7^{2 \times 4} = 7^8$

- Anything raised to the <u>power</u> <u>zero</u> is just 1, provided the number is not zero.
  $5^0 = 1$ $6^0 = 1$
  $2.7189^0 = 1$ $0^0 = $ undefined

- Anything to the <u>power 1</u> is just <u>itself</u>.
  $15^1 = 15$ $1923^1 = 1923$

The above rules also apply when the powers are negative.

EXAMPLES

$6^{-2} \times 6^{12} = 6^{-2+12} = 6^{10}$ $8^{-4} \times 8^{-3} = 8^{-4+-3} = 8^{-7}$

$(6^4)^{-2} = 6^{4 \times -2} = 6^{-8}$ $5^0 = 1$

INDICES AND ALGEBRA

The rules that apply with numbers also apply with letters.

LAWS OF INDICES

$$a^n \times a^m = a^{n+m}$$

$$a^n \div a^m = a^{n-m}$$

$$(a^n)^m = a^{n \times m}$$

$$a^0 = 1$$

$$a^1 = a$$

$$a^{-1} = \frac{1}{a}$$

Examiner's Top Tip
Indices are becoming a very common topic on the non-calculator paper — learn the rules and you should be OK!

EXAMPLES

$$4x^2 \times 3x^5 = 12x^7$$

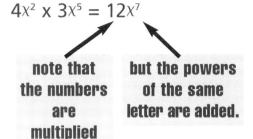
note that the numbers are multiplied — but the powers of the same letter are added.

$$12x^4 \div 3x^7 = 4x^{-3}$$
$$(7x^2)^2 = 49x^4$$
$$x^0 = 1$$
$$(2x^4)^3 = 8x^{12}$$

simplify
$$\frac{3x^7 \times 4x^9}{6x^4} = \frac{12x^{16}}{6x^4} = 2x^{12}$$

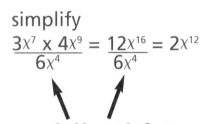
work this out in 2 stages

simplify
$$x^6 \times 4x^3 = 4x^9$$

simplify
$$\frac{12a^2b^3}{6a^3b^2} = \frac{2b}{a} \text{ or } 2a^{-1}b$$

simplify
$$\frac{4a^4b^3}{2ab} = 2a^3b^2$$

QUICK TEST

1. Simplify the following:

   a) $12^4 \times 12^8$ b) $9^{-2} \times 9^{-4}$ c) 4^0 d) $18^6 \div 18^{-2}$ e) $(4^2)^5$ f) 1^{20}

2. Simplify the following:

   a) $x^4 \times x^9$ b) $2x^6 \times 3x^7$ c) $12x^4 \div 3x^2$ d) $25x^9 \div 5x^{-2}$ e) $\dfrac{5x^6 \times 4x^9}{10x^3}$

1. a) 12^{12} b) 9^{-6} c) 1 d) 18^8 e) 4^{10} f) 1 2. a) x^{13} b) $6x^{13}$ c) $4x^2$ d) $5x^{11}$ e) $2x^{12}$

23

STANDARD INDEX FORM (OR STANDARD FORM)

Standard index form is used to write very large numbers or very small numbers in a simpler way. When written in standard form the number will be written as:

$$a \times 10^n$$

a must be between 1 and 10, $1 \leq a < 10$
The value of n is the number of times the decimal point has to move to the right to return the number to its original value.

Learn these three rules
1) The front number must always be between 1 and 10
2) The power of 10, n, is purely how far the decimal point moves
3) If the number is BIG   If the number is SMALL
    n is positive   n is negative

BIG NUMBERS

EXAMPLES
• Write 6230000 in standard form.
  Move the decimal point to between the 6 and 2 to give 6.230000 ($1 \leq 6.23 < 10$).
  Count how many places the decimal point needs to be moved to restore the number.
  6 2 3 0 0 0 0   (6 places)
  In standard form 6230000 = 6.23×10^6

  $4371 = 4.371 \times 10^3$ in standard form.

SMALL NUMBERS

EXAMPLES
• Write 0.00371 in standard form.
  Move the decimal point to between the 3 and 7 to give 3.71
  ($1 \leq 3.71 < 10$).
  Count how many places the decimal point has been moved.
  0.0 0 3 7 1 (3 places)
  In standard form $0.00371 = 3.71 \times 10^{-3}$

  This means that the decimal point is moved 3 places to the left.

  $0.0000479 = 4.79 \times 10^{-5}$ in standard form.

Watch Out!

Several common mistakes when answering standard form questions are:

• Reading a calculator display 2.4⁰⁷ incorrectly and writing down 2.4^7 instead of 2.4×10^7

• Forgetting to write the answer in standard form particularly on the non-calculator paper

e.g. $(2 \times 10^6) \times (6 \times 10^3)$ $= (2 \times 6) \times (10^6 \times 10^3)$

                                                $= 12 \times 10^9$

                                                $= 1.2 \times 10^{10}$

STANDARD FORM AND THE CALCULATOR

To key a number in standard form into the calculator, use the EXP key.
(Some calculators use EE. Make sure that you check your calculator,
as calculators vary greatly.)

EXAMPLES

6.23×10^6 can be keyed in as: $\quad 6 \ . \ 2 \ 3 \ EXP \ 6$

4.93×10^{-5} can be keyed in as: $\quad 4 \ . \ 9 \ 3 \ EXP \ 5 \ +/-$

Most calculators do not show standard form correctly on the display.

7.632^{09} means 7.632×10^9. 4.62^{-07} means 4.62×10^{-7}.

Remember to put in the x 10 part if it has been left out.

CALCULATIONS WITH STANDARD FORM

Use the calculator to do complex calculations in standard form.

EXAMPLES

$(2.6 \times 10^3) \times (8.9 \times 10^{12}) = 2.314 \times 10^{16}$

This would be keyed in as:

| 2 | . | 6 | EXP | 3 | x | 8 | . | 9 | EXP | 1 | 2 | = |

Just key in as normal:

| 2 | . | 7 | EXP | 3 | +/− |

Check that for $(1.8 \times 10^6) \div (2.7 \times 10^{-3})$ the answer is 6.6×10^8

If a calculation with standard form is on the non-calculator paper,
the laws of indices can be used when multiplying and dividing
numbers written in standard form.

EXAMPLES

$(2.4 \times 10^{-4}) \times (3 \times 10^7)$
$= (2.4 \times 3) \times (10^{-4} \times 10^7)$
$= 7.2 \times (10^{-4+7})$
$= 7.2 \times 10^3$

$(12.4 \times 10^{-4}) \div (4 \times 10^7)$
$= (12.4 \div 4) \times (10^{-4} \div 10^7)$
$= 3.1 \times (10^{-4-7})$
$= 3.1 \times 10^{-11}$

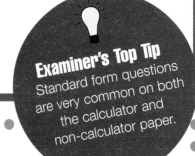

Examiner's Top Tip
Standard form questions
are very common on both
the calculator and
non-calculator paper.

QUICK TEST

1. **Write the following numbers in standard form:**

   a) 630000   b) 2730

   c) 0.0000429   d) 0.00000063

2. **Without a calculator work out the following, leaving your answer in standard form.**

   a) $(2 \times 10^5) \times (3 \times 10^7)$ b) $(6.1 \times 10^{12}) \times (2 \times 10^{-4})$

   c) $(8 \times 10^9) \div (2 \times 10^6)$ d) $(6 \times 10^8) \div (2 \times 10^{-10})$

3. **Work these out on a calculator. Give your answers to 3 s.f.**

   a) $\dfrac{1.279 \times 10^9}{2.94 \times 10^{-2}}$ b) $(1.693 \times 10^4) \times (2.71 \times 10^{12})$

4. **Calculate, giving your answers in standard form correct to 3 s.f.**

   $\dfrac{(3.72 \times 10^8) - (1.6 \times 10^4)}{3.81 \times 10^{-3}}$

4. 9.76×10^{10}

1. a) 6.3×10^5 b) 2.73×10^3 c) 4.29×10^{-5} d) 6.3×10^{-7} 2. a) 6×10^{12} b) 1.22×10^9 c) 4×10^3 d) 3×10^{18} 3. a) 4.35×10^{10} b) 4.59×10^{16}

EXAM QUESTIONS - Use the questions to test your progress. Check your answers on page 94.

1. From this list of numbers (2, 9, 21, 40, 41, 64, 100):
a) Write down the numbers that are odd ...9, 21, 41....................................
b) Write down the square numbers ....2, 9.................................
c) Write down the prime numbers ......2, 21, 41..............................
d) Write down any numbers which are factors of 80 ...2, 4, 8, 10, 20, 40.................
e) Write down any numbers which are multiples of 4 ...8, 16, 12.........................

2. The temperature outside is –6°, inside it is 15° warmer.
What is the temperature inside? ....

3. Work out the answers to:
a) 589 ×   b) 62 $\overline{)1674}$
      76
   $\overline{}$

....

4 Mohammed needs some tiles for the kitchen floor. The tiles are sold in boxes of 8. Mohammed works out
   that he needs 60 tiles. How many boxes will he need to buy?

....

(c) 5. Hussain scored 58 marks out of 75 in a test. What percentage did he get?

....

6. A school raises £525 at the summer fair. 60% of the money raised is used to repair the tennis courts.
How much is used to repair the tennis courts? ....

7. The ingredients for 8 small cakes are:
    • 300 g self-raising flour
    • 150 g butter
    • 250 g sugar
    • 2 eggs
   Andrew is making 20 small cakes. Write down the amounts of ingredients he will need.
   ....g self-raising flour
   ....g butter
   ....g sugar
   ....eggs

8. Mrs Patel inherits £55 000. She divides the money between her children in the ratio 3 : 3 : 5.
How much does the child with the largest share receive?
.... £55 000 ÷ 11 = £5000   3 × £5000 = £15000 ......
                                                                    £15000 : £15000 : £25000

(c) 9. Work these out on your calculator, giving your answers to 3 s.f.
a) $\dfrac{4.2\,(3.6 + 5.1)}{2 - 1.9}$ =   b) $\dfrac{3.8 + 4.6}{2.9 \times 4.1}$ =

....
....

10. Show how you would estimate the answer to this expression without using a calculator.
Work out the estimate.
      $\dfrac{8.7 + 9.02}{0.2 \times 48}$

....
....

(c) Indicates that a calculator may be used

(c) 11. Toothpaste is sold in three different sized tubes.
    ~50 ml = £1.24   75 ml = £1.96   100 ml = £2.42
Which of the tubes of toothpaste is the best value for money?
You must show full working out in order to justify your answer.

....

....

12. A piece of writing paper is 0.01 cm thick. A notepad has 150 sheets of paper.
How thick is the notepad?

....

....

(c) 13. The price of a CD player has been reduced by 15% in a sale. It now costs £320.
What was the original price?

....

....

(c) 14. A car was bought in 1997 for £9000. Each year it depreciates in value by 15%.
What is the car worth two years later?

....

....

(c) 15. James put £632 in a new savings account. At the end of every year interest at 4.2% is added to the amount
in his savings account at the beginning of that year.
Calculate the amount in James's savings account at the end of three years.

....

....

16. The price of a television has risen from £350 to £420.
Work out the percentage increase in the price

....

....

17. Write these numbers in standard form:
a) 2 670 000   b) 4270   c) 0.03296   d) 0.027

.......2.67×10^{6}............4.27×10^{3}..

....

....

....

(c) 18. The mass of a hair is 0.000042 g.
a) Write this number in standard form ....
b) Calculate, in standard form, the mass of 6×10^5 hairs ....

19. Work out the answers to these questions giving your answer in standard form:
a) $(2 \times 10^9) \times (6 \times 10^{12})$ ....
b) $(8 \times 10^9) \div (4 \times 10^{-2})$ ....

How did you do?

1–5	correct	....start again
6–10	correct	....getting there
11–15	correct	....good work
16–19	correct	....excellent

ALGEBRA ①
THIS INVOLVES USING LETTERS

ALGEBRAIC CONVENTIONS

- A <u>term</u> is a collection of numbers, letters and brackets, all multiplied together.
- Terms are separated by + and – signs. Each term has a + or – <u>attached</u> <u>to</u> <u>the</u> <u>front</u> <u>of</u> <u>it</u>.

$$3xy - 5r - 2x^2 + 4$$

invisible + sign xy term   r term x^2 term   number term

- 3 x a is written without the multiplication sign as 3a.
  a + a + a = 3a
  a x a x a = a^3, not 3a
  a x a x 2 = $2a^2$, not $(2a)^2$
  a x b x 2 = 2ab

COLLECTING LIKE TERMS

Expressions can be simplified by collecting <u>like</u> <u>terms</u>.
Only collect the terms if their letters and powers are <u>identical</u>.

Add the a terms together, then the terms with b. Remember a means 1a.

EXAMPLES

$4a + 2a = 6a$

$3a^2 + 6a^2 - 4a^2 = 5a^2$

$4a + 6b - 3a + 2b = a + 8b$

$9a + 4b$ cannot be simplified since there are no like terms.

$3xy + 2yx = 5xy$

Remember xy means the same as yx

WRITING FORMULAE

Quite often in the exam you are asked to write a formula when given some information or a diagram.

EXAMPLE
Frances buys x books at £2.50 each. She pays with a £20 note. If she receives C pounds change write down as a formula.

notice that no £ signs are put in our formula

$$C = 20 - 2.50x$$

this is the amount of money she spent

If in doubt check by substituting a value for x i.e: if she bought 1 book $x = 1$ so her change would be 20 – 2.50 x 1 = £17.50

EXAMPLE
Some patterns are made by using grey and white paving slabs.

Write a formula for the number of grey paving slabs (g) in a pattern that uses (w) white ones.

Formula is g = 2w + 2
2w represents the 2 layers, + 2 gives the grey slabs which are on either end of the white ones.

FORMULAE, EXPRESSIONS AND SUBSTITUTING

p + 3 is an <u>expression</u>.
y = p + 3 is a <u>formula</u>. The value of y depends on the value of p.
<u>Replacing</u> a <u>letter</u> <u>with</u> a <u>number</u> is <u>called</u> <u>substitution</u>. When substituting:
- Write out the expression first and then replace the letters with the values given.
- Work out the value on your calculator. Use bracket keys where possible and pay attention to the order of operations.

Try these out on your calculator

EXAMPLES

Using W = 5.6, t = –7.1 and $u = \frac{2}{5}$, find the value of these expressions, giving your answers to 3 s.f.

a) $\dfrac{W + t}{u}$ b) $W - \dfrac{t}{u}$ c) $\sqrt{Wt^2}$

Remember to show the substitution.

a) $\dfrac{W + t}{u} = \dfrac{5.6 + (-7.1)}{\frac{2}{5}} = -3.75$

b) $W - \dfrac{t}{u} = 5.6 - \dfrac{(-7.1)}{\frac{2}{5}} = 23.4$

c) $\sqrt{Wt^2} = \sqrt{5.6 \times (-7.1)^2} = 16.8$

You may need to treat t² as (-7.1)², depending on your calculator.

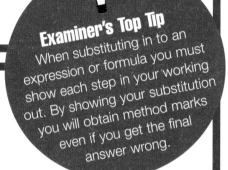

Examiner's Top Tip
When substituting in to an expression or formula you must show each step in your working out. By showing your substitution you will obtain method marks even if you get the final answer wrong.

USING FORMULAE

A formula describes the relationship between two (or more) variables.
A formula must have an = sign in it.

EXAMPLE

Andrew hires a van. There is a standing charge of £8 and then it costs £3 per hour. How much does it cost for:

a) 6 hours' drive
b) y hours' drive
c) Write a formula for the total hire cost C.

This is a formula which works out the cost of hiring the van for any number of hours.

a) $8 + (3 \times 6) = £26$
b) $8 + (3 \times y) = 8 + 3y$
d) $C = 8 + 3y$

QUICK TEST

1. Simplify these expressions by collecting like terms:

   a) 5a + 2a + 3a   *10a*

   b) 6a – 3b + 4b + 2a   *8a + b*

   c) 5x – 3x + 7x – 2y + 6y   *9x + 4y*

   d) $3xy^2 - 2x^2y + 6x^2y - 8xy^2$

2. Using p = 6.2, r = –3.2 and $s = \frac{2}{3}$, find the value of these expressions, giving your answer to 3 s.f.

   a) pr + s

   b) $p^2s - r$

   c) $r^2 - p/s$ d) $(ps - r)^2$

MULTIPLYING OUT BRACKETS

The subject of the formula is usually written first.

- This helps to simplify algebraic expressions.
- The term **outside** the brackets **multiplies** **each** **separate** **term** **inside** **the** **brackets**.

EXAMPLES

$3(2x + 5) = 6x + 15$ ($3 \times 2x = 6x$, $3 \times 5 = 15$)

$a(3a - 4) = 3a^2 - 4a$ $b(2a + 3b - c) = 2ab + 3b^2 - bc$

If the term outside the bracket is **negative**, all of the signs of the terms inside the bracket are **changed** when multiplying out.

EXAMPLES

$-4(2x + 3) = -8x - 12$ $-2(4 - 3x) = -8 + 6x$

To simplify expressions expand the brackets first then collect like terms.

EXAMPLES

Expand and simplify $2(x - 3) + x(x + 4)$.

$2(x - 3) + x(x + 4)$
$= 2x - 6 + x^2 + 4x$ Multiply out the brackets.
$= x^2 + 6x - 6$ Collect like terms.

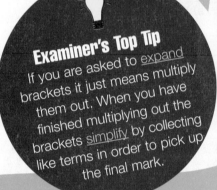

Examiner's Top Tip
If you are asked to <u>expand</u> brackets it just means multiply them out. When you have finished multiplying out the brackets <u>simplify</u> by collecting like terms in order to pick up the final mark.

MULTIPLICATION OF TWO BRACKETS

Each term in the first bracket is multiplied with each term in the second bracket.

Each term in the first bracket is multiplied with the second; simplify by collecting like terms.

EXAMPLES

Expand and simplify the following.

a) $(x + 2)(x + 3)$ $= x(x + 3) + 2(x + 3)$
                     $= x^2 + 3x + 2x + 6$
                     $= x^2 + 5x + 6$

b) $(2x + 4)(3x - 2) = 2x(3x - 2) + 4(3x - 2)$
                      $= 6x^2 - 4x + 12x - 8$
                      $= 6x^2 + 8x - 8$

c) $(x + y)^2$ $= x(x + y) + y(x + y)$
                     $= x^2 + xy + xy + y^2$
                     $= x^2 + 2xy + y^2$

A common error is to think that $(a + b)^2$ means $a^2 + b^2$.

(this is an identity; it is true for all values of x)

REARRANGING FORMULAE

The <u>subject</u> of a formula is the letter that appears on its own on one side of the formula.

EXAMPLES

Make p the subject of these formulae:
a) $r = (p + 6)^2$ b) $3(w + p) = 6p + 7$

a) $r = (p + 6)^2$ Deal with the power first. Take the square root of both sides.

$\sqrt{r} = p + 6$ Remove any terms added or subtracted.
               So subtract 6 from both sides.

$\sqrt{r} - 6 = p$ <u>or</u> $p = \sqrt{r} - 6$

(b) $3(w + p) = 6p + 7$ When the subject
   $3w + 3p = 6p + 7$ occurs twice, i.e. on
   $3w - 7 = 6p - 3p$ both sides of the
                     equals sign, they
   $3w - 7 = 3p$ need to be collected
                     onto one side, as
$p = \dfrac{3w - 7}{3}$ shown in the example.

FACTORISATION (PUTTING BRACKETS IN)

This is the reverse of expanding brackets. An expression is put into brackets by taking out common factors.

ONE BRACKET

$$y(x + 4) \xrightarrow{\text{expand}} xy + 4y$$
$$\xleftarrow{\text{factorise}}$$

To factorise $xy + 4y$:
- recognise that y is a factor of each term;
- take out the common factor;
- the expression is completed inside the bracket, so that the result is equivalent to $xy + 4y$, when multiplied out.

EXAMPLES
Factorise the following.
(a) $5x^2 + x = x(5x + 1)$
(b) $4x^2 + 8x = 4x(x + 2)$
(c) $5x^3 + 15x^4 = 5x^3(1 + 3x)$

Factorising can be useful when simplifying algebraic fractions.

EXAMPLE
Simplify $\dfrac{5x + 15}{(x + 3)} = \dfrac{5\cancel{(x + 3)}}{\cancel{(x + 3)}} = 5$

$$a = b^2 \qquad v^2 = 5^3 \times 5a$$

$$2(x - 3)$$

ALGEBRA ②

$$x = y^2$$

$$\frac{r = p^2}{q}$$

$$2(3 + x - 1) \qquad 3(y + x - 3)$$

FACTORISATION OF A QUADRATIC

TWO BRACKETS
Two brackets are obtained when a quadratic expression of the type $x^2 + bx + c$ is factorised.

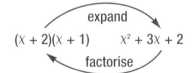

These multiply to give 2, and add to give 3 in $3x$

$$(x + 2)(x + 1) \xrightarrow{\text{expand}} x^2 + 3x + 2$$
$$\xleftarrow{\text{factorise}}$$

EXAMPLES
Factorise the following.
a) $x^2 + 5x - 6 = (x - 1)(x + 6)$
b) $x^2 - 6x + 8 = (x - 2)(x - 4)$
c) $x^2 - 25 = (x - 5)(x + 5)$

this is known as the difference of two squares. In general $x^2 - a^2 = (x - a)(x + a)$.

QUICK TEST

1. Multiply out the brackets and simplify where possible:

   a) $3(x + 2)$ b) $2(x + y)$

   c) $-3(2x + 4)$ d) $(x + 2)(x + 3)$

   e) $(y - 4)(y - 3)$ f) $(a + 2)^2$

2. Factorise the following expressions:

   a) $3x + 6$ b) $5y - 15$

   c) $12x^2 - 6x$ d) $x^2 - 5x - 6$

   e) $x^2 - 3x + 2$ f) $x^2 - 16$

3. Make u the subject of the formula

   $v^2 = u^2 + 2as$.

SOLVING LINEAR EQUATIONS OF THE FORM $ax + b = c$

When solving equations, the balance method is used; whatever is done to one side of the equation must be done to the other.

EXAMPLE

Solve
$$2x + 15 = 9$$
$$2x = 9 - 15 \quad \text{Subtract 15 from both sides.}$$
$$2x = -6$$
$$x = -6 \div 2 \quad \text{Divide both sides by 2.}$$
$$x = -3$$

EQUATIONS 1

AN EQUATION INVOLVES AN UNKNOWN VALUE WHICH HAS TO BE WORKED OUT

SOLVING LINEAR EQUATIONS OF THE FORM $ax + b = cx + d$

The trick with this type of equation is to get the x's together on one side of the equal sign and the numbers on the other side.

EXAMPLE

Solve:
$$5x-9 = 12-4x$$
$$9x-9 = 12 \quad \text{add } 4x \text{ to both sides.}$$
$$9x = 21 \quad \text{Add 9 to both sides.}$$
$$x = \tfrac{21}{9} = 2\tfrac{1}{3} \quad \text{If in the exam you do not know that } \tfrac{21}{9} = 2\tfrac{1}{3},$$
$$\text{leave it as } \tfrac{21}{9} \text{ to obtain full marks!}$$

SOLVING QUADRATIC EQUATIONS

Make sure the quadratic equation is equal to zero. Then factorise the quadratic equation.

EXAMPLES

Solve the following:

a) $x^2 - 5x = 0$ x is a common factor.
   $x(x - 5) = 0$
   Either $x = 0$ or $x - 5 = 0$, i.e. $x = 5$

b) $x^2 - 3x = 10$
   $x^2 - 3x - 10 = 0$ Make it equal to zero and factorise.
   $(x + 2)(x - 5) = 0$
   Either $(x + 2) = 0$, i.e. $x = -2$, or $(x - 5) = 0$, i.e. $x = 5$

SOLVING LINEAR EQUATIONS WITH BRACKETS

Just because an equation has brackets don't be put off. It's just the same as the other equations once the brackets have been multiplied out.

EXAMPLES

a) Solve:

$$3(x - 2) = 2(x + 6)$$
$$3x - 6 = 2x + 12$$
$$x - 6 = 12$$
$$x = 18$$

Multiply out the brackets first.

b) Solve:

$$5(x - 2) + 6 = 3(x - 4) + 10$$
$$5x - 10 + 6 = 3x - 12 + 10$$
$$5x - 4 = 3x - 2$$
$$2x = 2$$
$$x = 1$$

USING EQUATIONS TO SOLVE PROBLEMS

EXAMPLE

The perimeter of the triangle is 20 cm. Work out the value of x and hence find the length of the 3 sides.

$$x + 2x + 5 + 4x + 1 = 20$$

$$7x + 6 = 20$$
$$7x = 20 - 6$$
$$7x = 14$$
$$x = \frac{14}{7}$$
$$x = 2$$

The perimeter is found by adding lengths together. Collect like terms. Solve the equation as before.

So the lengths of the sides are 2 (= x), 9 (= 4x + 1) and 9 (= 2x + 5)

QUICK TEST

Solve the following equations:

1. $\frac{x}{2} - 3 = 9$

2. $4x + 2 = 20$

3. $5x + 3 = 2x + 9$

4. $6x - 1 = 15 + 2x$

5. $3(x + 2) = x + 4$

6. $2(x - 1) = 6(2x + 2)$

7. $x^2 + 4x - 5 = 0$

8. $x^2 - 5x + 6 = 0$

Examiner's Top Tip
Solving equations is a very common topic at GCSE. Try to work through them in a logical way always showing full working out. If you have time check your answer by substituting it back into the equation to see if it works.

1. $x = 24$ 2. $x = 4.5$ 3. $x = 2$ 4. $x = 4$ 5. $x = -1$ 6. $x = -1.4$ 7. $x = 1, x = -5$ 8. $x = 2, x = 3$

ALGEBRA

SIMULTANEOUS EQUATIONS

Two equations with two unknowns are called <u>simultaneous</u> <u>equations</u>.
They can be solved in several ways. Solving equations simultaneously involves finding values for the letters that will make both equations work.

GRAPHICAL METHOD
The points at which any two graphs intersect represent the simultaneous solutions of these equations.

EXAMPLE
Solve the simultaneous equations $y = 2x - 1$, $x + y = 5$
• Draw the two graphs.

$y = 2x - 1$ If $x = 0$, $y = -1$
             If $y = 0$, $x = \frac{1}{2}$
$x + y = 5$ If $x = 0$, $y = 5$
             If $x = 0$, $x = 5$
• At the point of intersection $x = 2$ and $y = 3$.

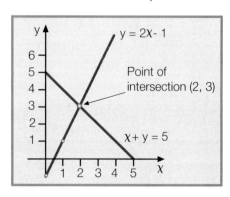

ELIMINATION METHOD
If the coefficient of one of the letters is the same in both equations, then that letter may be eliminated by subtracting the equations.

EXAMPLE
Solve simultaneously

$$2x + 3y = 6$$
$$x + y = 1$$

STEP 1
Label the equations ① and ②.

$2x + 3y = 6$ ①
$x + y = 1$ ②

STEP 2
Since no coefficients match multiply equation ② by 2. Rename it equation ③.

$2x + 3y = 6$ ①
$2x + 2y = 2$ ③

> The coefficient is the number a letter is multiplied by, e.g. the coefficient of −2x is −2.

STEP 3
The coefficient of x in equations ① and ③ are the same. Subtract equation ③ from equation ① and then solve the remaining equation.

$0x + y = 4$
$\therefore y = 4$

STEP 4
Substitute the value of $y = 4$ into equation ① or equation ②. Solve this equation to find x.

$x + 4 = 1$
$x = 1 - 4$
$x = -3$

STEP 5
Check in equation ①.

$(2 x - 3) + (3 x 4) = 6$

The solution is $x = -3$, $y = 4$

> **Examiner's Top Tip**
> Simultaneous equations are usually a difficult topic to master. Try to learn the steps outlined above and practise lots of examples. Use the check at the end to make sure that you have the correct answers.

Remember: To eliminate terms with opposite signs, add the equations
To eliminate terms with the same signs, subtract the equations.

34

SOLVING CUBIC EQUATIONS BY TRIAL AND IMPROVEMENT

Trial and improvement gives an approximate solution to equations.

EXAMPLE
The equation $x^3 - 5x = 10$ has a solution between 2 and 3. Find this solution to 2 decimal places.

Draw a table to help.
Substitute different values of x into $x^3 - 5x$.

Examiner's Top Tip
Make sure you write down the solution of x, not the answer to $x^3 - 5x$.

x	$x^3 - 5x$	Comment
2.5	3.125	too small
2.8	7.952	too small
2.9	9.889	too small
2.95	10.922375	too big
2.94	10.712184	too big
2.91	10.092171	too big

At this stage the solution is trapped between 2.90 and 2.91. Checking the middle value $x = 2.905$ gives $x^3 - 5x = 9.99036 \ldots$ which is too small.

```
    2.90                    2.905                   2.91
(too small)             (too small)             (too big)
```

The diagram makes it clear that the solution is 2.91 correct to two decimal places.

EQUATIONS ②

• •

QUICK TEST

1. Solve the following pairs of simultaneous equations:

   a) $4x + 7y = 10$ b) $3a - 5b = 1$
      $2x + 3y = 3$ $2a + 3b = 7$

2. The diagram shows the graphs of the equations $x + y = 2$ and $y = x - 4$.
   Use the diagram to solve the simultaneous equations.
   $x + y = 2$
   $y = x - 4$

3. The equation $y^3 + y = 40$ has a solution between 3 and 4.
   Find this solution to 1 d.p. by using a method of trial and improvement.

INEQUALITIES

THE 4 INEQUALITY SYMBOLS

> means 'greater than' $\geq$ means 'greater than or equal to'
< means 'less than' $\leq$ means 'less than or equal to'
So $x > 3$ and $3 < x$ both say 'x is greater than 3'

Inequalities are solved in a similar way to equations. **Multiplying and dividing by negative numbers** changes the **direction** of the sign. For example if $- x \geq 5$ then $x \leq -5$.

EXAMPLES
Solve the following inequalities:

a) $4x - 2 < 2x + 6$
   $2x - 2 < 6$ Subtract $2x$ from both sides.
   $2x < 8$ Add 2 to both sides.
   $x < 4$ Divide both sides by 2.

The solution of the inequality may be represented on a number line.

Use • when the end point is included and **o** when the end point is not included.

b) $-5 < 3x + 1 \leq 13$ Subtract 1 from each part.
   $-6 < 3x \leq 12$ Divide by 3.
   $-2 < x \leq 4$

The <u>integer values</u> which satisfy the above inequality are

$-1, 0, 1, 2, 3, 4.$

GRAPHS OF INEQUALITIES

The graph of an equation such as y = 3 is a line, whereas the graph of the inequality y < 3 is a region which has the line y = 3 as its **boundary**.

To show the region for given inequalities:

• Draw the boundary lines first.

• For **strict** inequalities > and <, the boundary line is not included and is shown as a dotted line.

• It is often easier with several inequalities to shade out the unwanted regions, so that the solution is shown **unshaded**.

EXAMPLE
The diagram shows unshaded the region $x > 1$, $x + y \leq 4$, $y \geq 0$

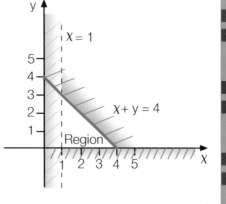

Examiner's Top Tip
Inequalities are solved in a similar way to equations.

QUICK TEST

Solve the following inequalities:

1. $2x - 3 < 9$

2. $5x + 1 \geq 21$

3. $1 \leq 3x - 2 \leq 7$

4. $1 \leq 5x + 2 < 12$

1. $x < 6$ 2. $x \geq 4$ 3. $1 \leq x \leq 3$ 4. $-\frac{1}{5} \leq x < 2$

NUMBER PATTERNS AND SEQUENCES

Examiner's Top Tip
Check your rule for the nth term works, by substituting another value of n into your expression.

A <u>sequence</u> is a list of numbers. There is usually a relationship between the numbers. Each value in the list is called a <u>term</u>.

EXAMPLE
The odd numbers form a sequence 1, 3, 5, 7, 9, 11, . . . in which the terms have a <u>common</u> <u>difference</u> of 2.

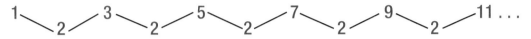

The common difference is 2

IMPORTANT NUMBER SEQUENCES
Square numbers	1, 4, 9, 16, 25, . . .
Cube numbers	1, 8, 27, 64, 125, . . .
Triangular numbers	1, 3, 6, 10, 15, . . .
The Fibonacci sequence	1, 1, 2, 3, 5, 8, 13, . . .

FINDING THE NTH TERM OF A LINEAR SEQUENCE

The nth term is often denoted by U_n. For example, the 12th term is U_{12}.
For a linear sequence, the nth term takes the form
$U_n = an + b$.

EXAMPLE
For the sequence of odd numbers, find an expression for the nth term.
1, 3, 5, 7, 9, . . .

- Find the common difference; this is a.
  So a = 2 here. So $U_n = 2n + b$.
- Now substitute the values of U_1 and n.
  n = 1 and $U_1 = 1$.
  This gives 1 = 2 + b.
  So b = –1.
- nth term: $U_n = 2n – 1$.
- Check: for the 10th term $U_{10} = 2 \times 10 – 1 = 19$.

THE NTH TERM OF QUADRATIC SEQUENCE

For a quadratic sequence the first differences are not constant but the second differences are.

The nth term takes the form
$U_n = an^2 + bn + c$,
where b, c may be zero.

Finding the nth term of a quadratic sequence is a useful technique for when you are carrying out Investigational tasks for coursework

EXAMPLE
Find the nth term of 3, 9, 19, 33

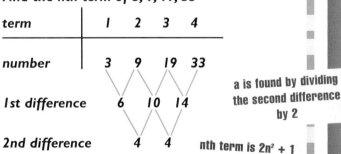

term	1	2	3	4
number	3	9	19	33
1st difference		6	10	14
2nd difference			4	4

a is found by dividing the second difference by 2

nth term is $2n^2 + 1$

QUICK TEST

1. Write down the next two terms in the sequences below:

   a) 5, 7, 9, 11, <u>13</u> , <u>15</u>   b) 1, 4, 9, 16, <u>25</u>, <u>36</u>   c) 12, 10, 8, 6, <u>4</u> , <u>2</u>

2. Write down the nth term in the sequences below:

   a) 5, 7, 9, 11 . . .   b) 2, 5, 8, 11 . . .   c) 6, 10, 14, 18 . . .   d) 8, 6, 4, 2 . . .

1. a) 13, 15 b) 25, 36 c) 4, 2   2. a) 2n + 3 b) 3n – 1 c) 4n + 2 d) 10 – 2n

DRAWING STRAIGHT LINE GRAPHS

In order to draw a straight line graph follow these easy steps:-

STEP 1
Choose 3 values of x and draw up a table.

STEP 2
Work out the value of y for each value of x.

STEP 3
Plot the coordinates and join up the points with a straight line.

STEP 4
Label the graph.

EXAMPLE
Draw the graph of $y = 3x - 1$
1. Draw up a table with some suitable values of x.

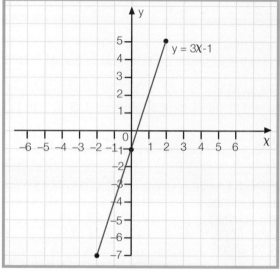

x	−2	0	2
y	−7	−1	5

2. Work out the y values by putting each x value into the equation.
e.g. $x = -2$ ∴ $y = 3 \times -2 - 1$
$= -6 - 1$
$= -7$

3. Plot the points and draw the line.

STRAIGHT LINE GRAPHS

FINDING THE GRADIENT OF A LINE

Do not count the squares as the scale may be different

• To find the gradient, choose two points.
• Draw a triangle as shown.
• Find the change in y (height) and the change in x (base).
• gradient = $\frac{\text{change in y}}{\text{change in } x}$ or $\frac{\text{height}}{\text{base}} = \frac{4}{3} = 1\frac{1}{3}$
• Decide if the gradient is positive or negative.

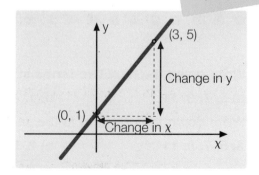

GRAPHS OF Y = a, X = b

y = a is a horizontal line with every y coordinate equal to a.

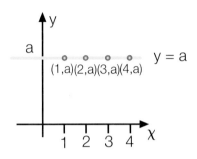

X = b is a vertical line with every X coordinate equal to b.

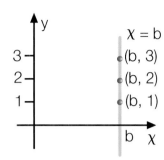

INTERPRETING y = mX + c

The general equation of a straight line graph is $y = mX + c$.

m is the gradient (steepness) of the line.

· As m increases the line gets steeper.
· If m is positive the line slopes forwards.
· If m is negative the line slopes backwards.

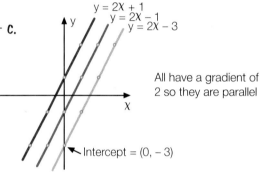

All have a gradient of 2 so they are parallel

Intercept = (0, – 3)

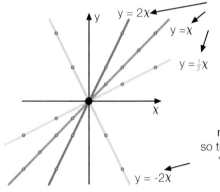

As m increases the line gets steeper

m is negative so the graph slopes 'backwards'.

c is the intercept on the y axis, that is, where the graph cuts the y axis.

Parallel lines have the same gradient.

Examiner's Top Tip
You need to be able to sketch a straight line graph from its equation. If you can do this then you will be able to tell if the graph you have drawn is correct.

***

QUICK TEST

1. Draw the graph of $y = 6 - 2X$. From your graph write down the solution of the equations:

   a) $6 - 2X = 4$

   b) $6 - 2X = 3$

2. Write down the gradient and intercept for each of these straight line graphs:

   a) $y = 4 + 2X$ b) $y = 3X - 2$ c) $2y = 6X + 4$

CURVED GRAPHS

GRAPHS INVOLVING x^3 AND $\frac{1}{x}$

GRAPHS INVOLVING x^3

An equation of the form

$y = ax^3 + bx^2 + cx + d$

is called a <u>cubic</u> where $a \neq 0$. For $a > 0$ the graph of a cubic takes one of these forms.

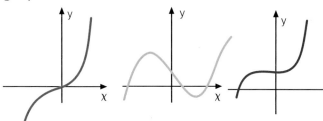

For $a < 0$ the overall trend is reversed.

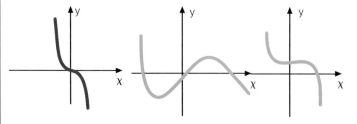

GRAPHS INVOLVING $\frac{1}{x}$

An equation of the form $y = a/x$ takes two basic forms depending on the value of a.

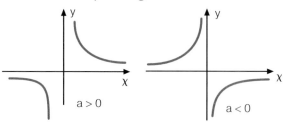

Examiner's Top Tip
Show clearly on your graph how you have taken the reading.

EXAMPLE

Draw the graph of $P = \frac{18}{V}$ for values of V from 1 to 6. Find the value of V if $P = 8$.

• Draw the table of values first

V	1	2	3	4	5	6
P	18	9	6	4.5	3.6	3

• Find the values of P by dividing 18 by V.
• Draw a smooth curve through the points.
• To find V when $P = 8$ read across at $P = 8$ then draw a line down. $V = 2.25$.

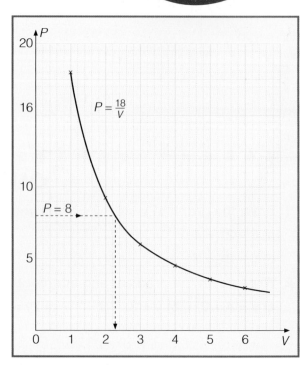

GRAPHS OF THE FORM $y = ax^2 + bx + c$

These are called **<u>quadratic graphs</u>** where a ≠ 0.
These graphs are curved.
If a > 0 then the graph is U-shaped.

If a < 0 then the graph is an upside-down U.

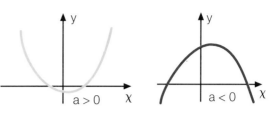

a > 0   X   a < 0   X

They are often known as parabolas.

EXAMPLE
Draw the graph of $y = x^2 - x - 6$ using values of X from –2 to 3.
Use the graph to find the value of X when y = –3.
• Make a table of values.

x = 0.5 is worked out to find the minimum value.

X	–2	–1	0	1	2	3	0.5
y	0	–4	–6	–6	–4	0	–6.25

• To work out the values of y substitute the values of X into the equation:
    e.g. If X = 1 $y = x^2 - x - 6$
                       $= 1^2 - 1 - 6$
                       $= -6$
• Don't try and punch this all into your calculator at once.
    Do it step by step.
• Plot the points and join them with a **<u>smooth</u>** curve.

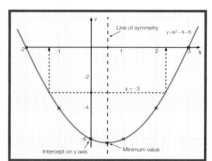

• The minimum value is when X = 0.5, y = –6.25.
• The line of symmetry is at X = 0.5.
• The curve cuts the y axis at (0, –6), i.e. (0, c).
• When y = –3, read across from y = –3 to the graph then read
    up to the X axis. X = 2.3 and X = –1.3. These are the approximate
    solutions of the equation $x^2 - x - 6 = -3$.

Show clearly on your graph how you take your readings.

***

QUICK TEST

Examiner's Top Tip
Draw the curve with a sharp pencil, go through all the points and check for any parts that look wrong.
this point is obviously wrong

1. a) Complete the table of values for the graph $y = x^3 + 3$.

X	–3	–2	–1	0	1	2	3
y							

b) Draw the graph of $y = x^3 + 3$. Use scales of 2 unit per 1 cm on
    the X axis and 20 units per 1 cm on the y axis.

c) From the graph find the value of x when y = 15

2. Match each of the four graphs below with one of the following equations:

    a) $y = 2x - 5$ b) $y = x^2 + 3$ c) $y = 3 - x^2$ d) $y = 5 - x$ e) $y = x^3$ f) $y = \frac{2}{x}$

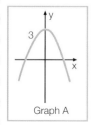

Graph A

Graph B

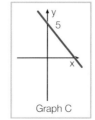

Graph C

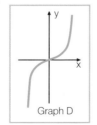

Graph D

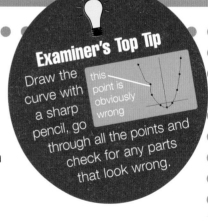

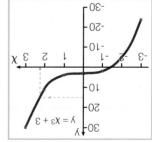

$y = x^3 + 3$

GRAPHS IN PRACTICAL SITUATIONS

Linear graphs are often used to show relationships.

EXAMPLE
The graph shows the charges made by a van hire firm.
• Point A shows how much was charged for hiring the van, i.e. £50.
• The gradient = 20.
  This means that £20 was charged per day for the hire of the van. Hence for 5 days' hire the van cost £50 + £20 x 5 = £150

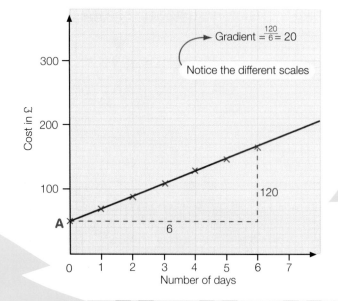

DISTANCE–TIME GRAPHS

These are often called travel graphs.
The speed of an object can be found by finding the gradient of the line.

speed = $\dfrac{\text{distance travelled}}{\text{time taken}}$

EXAMPLE
The graph shows Mr Rogers' car journey. Work out the speed of each stage.
a) The car is travelling at 30 m.p.h. for 1 hour (30 ÷ 1).
b) The car is stationary for 30 minutes.
c) The graph is steeper so the car is travelling faster, at a speed of 60 m.p.h. for 30 minutes (30 ÷ 0.5).
d) The car is stationary for 1 hour.
e) The return journey is at a speed of 40 m.p.h. (60 ÷ 1.5).

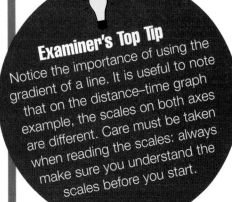

Examiner's Top Tip
Notice the importance of using the gradient of a line. It is useful to note that on the distance–time graph example, the scales on both axes are different. Care must be taken when reading the scales: always make sure you understand the scales before you start.

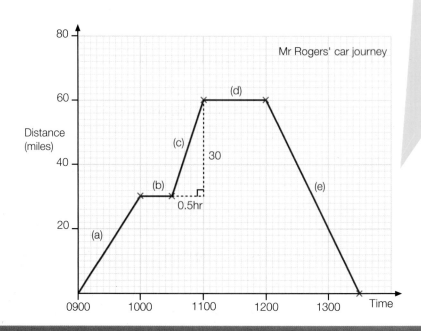

CONVERSION GRAPHS

These are used to convert values of one quantity to another, e.g. litres to pints, km to miles, £ to dollars, etc.

EXAMPLE
Suppose £1 is worth $1.50.
Draw a conversion graph.

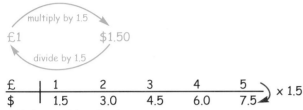

£	1	2	3	4	5
$	1.5	3.0	4.5	6.0	7.5

$\times 1.5$

· Make a table of values.
· Plot each of these points on the graph paper.
· To change $ to £, read across to the line then down,
  e.g. $4 is £2.67 (approx.)
· To change £ to $, read up to the line then read across,
  e.g. £4.50 is $6.80 (approx.)

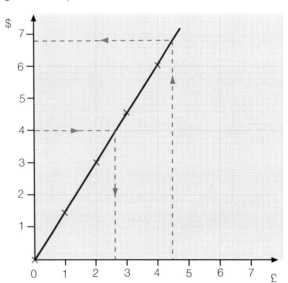

INTERPRETING GRAPHS

QUICK TEST

1.
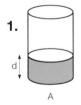 
   A   B   C

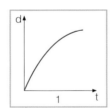 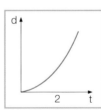 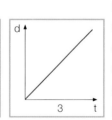
   1   2   3

These containers are being filled with a liquid at a rate of 150 ml per second. The graphs show how the depth of the water changes with time.
Match the containers with the graphs.

2. The travel graph shows the car journeys of two people. From the travel graph find:

a) the speed at which Miss Young is travelling.

b) the length of time Mr Price has a break

c) the speed of Mr Price from London to Birmingham.

d) the time at which Miss Young and Mr Price pass each other.

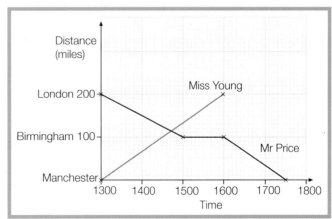

1. Write down a formula for the total cost T in pence of y balloons at 85 pence each and 8 party poppers at z pence each.

....

2. Here are some patterns made out of matchsticks:

1   2   3   4

a) In the space provided draw pattern 4
The table shows the number of matchsticks needed for pattern 1 to pattern 3.
b) Complete the table
c) How many matchsticks
   are needed for pattern 100? ....
d) Write down a formula connecting
   the pattern number (p) and the
   number of matchsticks (m) ....

....

Pattern number	Number of matchsticks
1	4
2	7
3	10
4	
5	
6	

3. Solve the following equations
a) $2x + 4 = 10$ b) $3x - 1 = 11$ c) $5x - 3 = 2x + 12$ d) $3(x + 1) = 9$ e) $2(x + 1) = x + 3$
   3   4   5   2   ?
....

4. The perimeter of the triangle is 22 cm:
a) Write down an equation for the perimeter
   of the triangle ....
b) Use your equation to find the length of the
   shortest side of the triangle ....

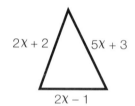

2X + 2   5X + 3

2X – 1

5. a) Complete the table of values for $y = 3x - 4$

X		–2	–1	0	1	2	3
$y = 3x - 4$							

b) On graph paper plot your values for x and y. Join your points with a straight line
c) Write down the coordinates of the points where your line crosses the x-axis.

....

6. Here are the first five terms of a number sequence: 3, 9, 19, 33, 51.
Write down an expression for the nth term of the sequence.

....

7. Simplify:
a) $3x^2 \times 4x^2$ ....
b) $6x^2 y \times 2x^3 y^2$ ....
c) $12y^4 \div 3y$ ....
d) $(3y^2)^2$ ....

8. Solve the simultaneous equations:
$4a + 3b = 6$ ....
$2a - 3b = 12$ ....

 Indicates that a calculator may be used

c) 9. $P^2 = 5\chi y - 3\chi^2$

a) Calculate the value of P when $\chi = 5.8$, $y = 105$ ....

b) Rearrange the formula $P^2 = 5\chi y - 3\chi^2$ to make y the subject.............................

c) 10. The equation $\chi^3 - 2\chi = 2$ has a solution between 2 and 3.

By using a method of trial and improvement, find this solution to one decimal place.

....

11. Solve the inequality $2 \leq 5n - 3 \leq 12$.

....

12. Match the graphs with the equations.

i) $y = \chi^2 - 4$ ii) $y = 2\chi + 1$ iii) $y = 3 - 4\chi$ iv) $\chi y = 6$

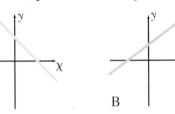
A

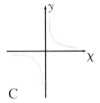
B

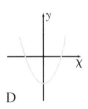
C

D

....

13. Water is being poured into these containers at a rate of 250 ml per second. The graphs below show how the height of the water changes with time. Match the containers with the graphs.

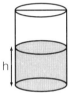
A

B

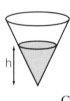
C

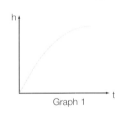
Graph 1

Graph 2

Graph 3

14. A drive has the dimensions as shown in the diagram

a) Write down an expression, in terms of g, for the area in m^2 of the drive.

....

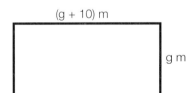
(g + 10) m

g m

b) Given that the area of the drive is 11 m^2,

show that $g^2 + 10g = 11$.

....

c) Solve the quadratic equation and find the length and width of the drive.

....

How did you do?

1–5	correct	....start again
6–9	correct	....getting there
10–12	correct	....good work
13–14	correct	....excellent

45

2D SHAPES

QUADRILATERALS

These are four-sided shapes.

TRIANGLES

There are several types of triangle.

Equilateral
3 sides equal.
3 angles equal.

Isosceles
2 sides equal.
Base angles equal.
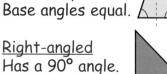

Right-angled
Has a 90° angle.

Scalene
No sides or angles the same.

Square
4 lines of symmetry.
Rotational symmetry of order 4.
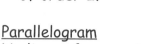

Rectangle
2 lines of symmetry.
Rotational symmetry of order 2.

Parallelogram
No lines of symmetry.
Rotational symmetry of order 2.

Rhombus
2 lines of symmetry.
Rotational symmetry of order 2.

Kite
1 line of symmetry.
No rotational symmetry.

Trapezium
Isosceles trapezium:
1 line of symmetry.
No rotational symmetry.

3D SOLIDS

 Cube

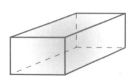 Cuboid

Square-based pyramid

Triangular-based pyramid (tetrahedron)

 Cylinder

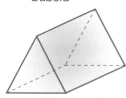 Triangular prism

 Cone

 Sphere

NETS OF SOLIDS

If you were making the shape you would need tabs for sticking.

The net of a 3D shape is the 2D shape which is folded to make the 3D shape.

EXAMPLES

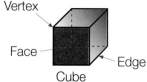
Vertex
Face
Edge
Cube

Square-based pyramid

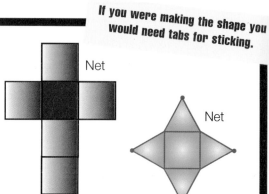
Net

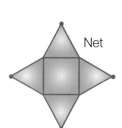
Net

PLANS AND ELEVATIONS

A plan is what is seen if a 3D shape is looked down on from above.
An elevation is seen if the 3D shape is looked at from the side, or front.

Examiner's Top Tip
When drawing plans and elevations of 3D shapes, measure and draw them carefully.

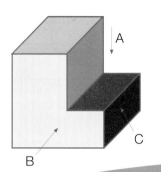

Plan

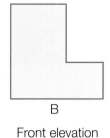

Front elevation

Side elevation

SHAPES AND SOLIDS

THE CIRCLE

Diameter = 2 x radius

The **circumference** is the distance around the outside edge.

A **chord** is a line that joins two points on the circumference. The line does not go through the centre.

A **tangent** touches the circle at one point only.

An **arc** is part of the circumference.

A **sector** of a circle is the area bounded by two radii and an arc.

A **segment** of a circle is the area bounded by a chord and an arc.

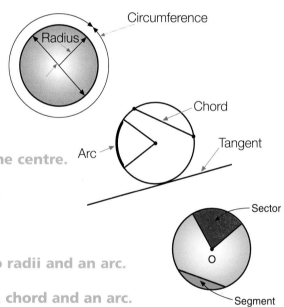

QUICK TEST

1. Draw a quick sketch of the main 3D shapes and give them their mathematical names (you need to know 8).
2. Draw a quick sketch of the main quadrilaterals and give them their mathematical names.
3. Draw the net of this cuboid.

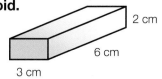

2 cm

6 cm

3 cm

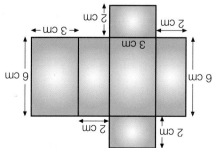

1. and 2. Crosscheck with information given on these pages   3. See diagram below

SHAPES AND SOLIDS

47

SYMMETRY

REFLECTIVE SYMMETRY

Both sides of a symmetrical shape are the same when a mirror line is drawn across it. The mirror line is known as the **line** or **axis of symmetry**.

1 line

1 line

3 lines

No lines

ROTATIONAL SYMMETRY

A 2D (two-dimensional) shape has rotational symmetry if, when turned, it looks exactly the same. The order of rotational symmetry is the number of times the shape turns and looks the same. For the letter M the shape has 1 position. It is said to have rotational symmetry of order 1, or no rotational symmetry.

Order 1

Order 1

Order 3

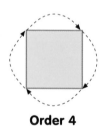

Order 4

PLANE SYMMETRY

This is symmetry in 3D (three-dimensional) solids only.

A 3D shape has a plane of symmetry if the plane divides the shape into two halves, and one half is an exact mirror image of the other.

Plane of symmetry

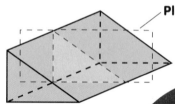

Examiner's Top Tip

When asked to draw in a plane of symmetry on a solid, make sure that it is a closed shape – don't just draw in a line of symmetry.

QUICK TEST

1. What are the names of the three types of symmetry?

2. The dashed lines are the lines of symmetry. Complete the shape so that it is symmetrical.

3. Draw a plane of symmetry on this solid.

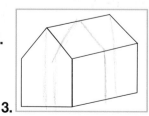

3.

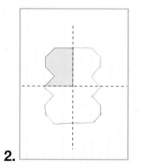

2.

CONSTRUCTIONS

CONSTRUCTING A TRIANGLE

EXAMPLE

Use compasses to construct this triangle.
- Draw the longest side AB.
- With the compass point at A, draw an arc of radius 4 cm.
- With the compass point at B, draw an arc of radius 5 cm.
- Join A and B to the point where the two arcs meet at C.

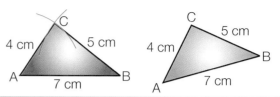

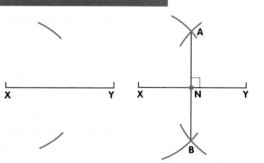

THE PERPENDICULAR BISECTOR OF A LINE

- Draw a line XY.
- Draw two arcs with the compasses, using X as the centre. The compasses must be set at a radius greater than half the distance of XY.
- Draw two more arcs with Y as the centre. (Keep the compasses the same distance apart as before.)
- Join the two points where the arcs cross.
- AB is the perpendicular bisector of XY.
- N is the midpoint of XY.

THE PERPENDICULAR FROM A POINT TO A LINE

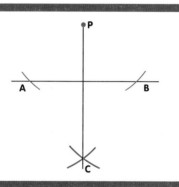

- From P draw arcs to cut the line at A and B.
- From A and B draw arcs with the same radius to intersect at C.
- Join P to C; this line is perpendicular to AB.

BISECTING AN ANGLE

- Draw two lines XY and YZ to meet at an angle.
- Using compasses, place the point at Y and draw arcs on XY and YZ.
- Place the compass point at the two arcs on XY and YZ and draw arcs to cross at N. Join Y and N. YN is the bisector of angle XYZ.

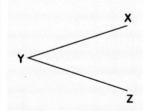

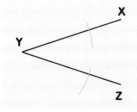

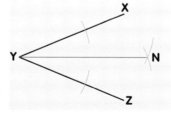

Examiner's Top Tip
Constructions are useful when answering locus questions and questions on scale drawings.

QUICK TEST

1. **Bisect this angle.** ➡
2. **Draw the perpendicular bisector of a 10 cm line.**

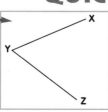

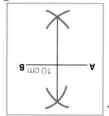

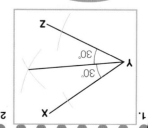

ANGLE FACTS

Angles on a straight line add up to <u>180°</u>.
a + b + c = 180°

Angles at a <u>point</u> add up to <u>360°</u>.
a + b + c + d = 360°

Angles in a <u>triangle</u> add up to <u>180°</u>.
a + b + c = 180°

Angles in a <u>quadrilateral</u> add up to 360°.
a + b + c+ d = 360°

<u>Vertically</u> <u>opposite</u> angles are <u>equal</u>.
a = b, c = d
a + d = b + c = 180°

An <u>exterior</u> <u>angle</u> of a triangle equals the sum of the <u>two</u> opposite <u>interior</u> <u>angles</u>.
a + b = c

ANGLES

READING ANGLES

When asked to find XYZ or ∠XYZ or XŶZ, find the <u>middle letter</u> angle, angle Y.

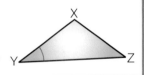

ANGLES IN PARALLEL LINES

<u>Alternate</u> (z) angles are <u>equal</u>.

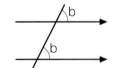

Corresponding angles are <u>equal</u>.

Supplementary angles add up to 180°. c + d = 180°

EXAMPLES
Find the angles labelled by letters.

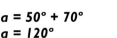

a = 50° + 70°
a = 120°

a + 80° + 40° + 85° = 360°
a = 360° − 205°
a = 155°

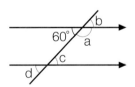

a = 120° (angles on a straight line)
b = 60° (vertically opposite)
c = 60° (corresponding to b)
d = 60° (vertically opposite to c)

POLYGONS

These are 2D shapes with <u>straight</u> sides.
<u>Regular</u> <u>polygons</u> are shapes with all sides and angles equal.

Number of sides	Name of polygon
3	Triangle
4	Quadrilateral
5	Pentagon
6	Hexagon
7	Heptagon
8	Octagon
9	Nonagon
10	Decagon

TESSELLATIONS

A <u>tessellation</u> is a pattern of 2D shapes which fit together without leaving any gaps.
For shapes to tessellate, the angles at each point must add up to 360°.

EXAMPLE
Regular pentagons will not tessellate.
Each interior angle is 108°, and
3 x 108° = 324°.
A gap of 360° – 324° = 36° is left.

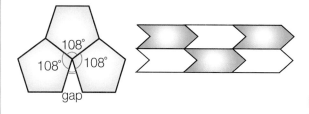

 AN ACUTE ANGLE IS BETWEEN 0° AND 90°.

 AN OBTUSE ANGLE IS BETWEEN 90° AND 180°.

 A REFLEX ANGLE IS BETWEEN 180° AND 360°.

 A RIGHT ANGLE IS 90°.

ANGLES IN A POLYGON

There are two types of angle in a polygon: interior (inside) and exterior (outside).
For a regular polygon with n sides:
- sum of exterior angles = 360°, so exterior angle = $\frac{360°}{n}$
- interior angle + exterior angle = 180°
- sum of interior angles = (n – 2) x 180° or (2n – 4) x 90°

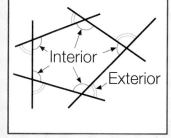

EXAMPLE
A regular polygon has an interior angle of 150°.
How many sides does it have? Let n be the number of sides.
exterior + interior = 180°
exterior angle = 180° – 150° = 30°
But exterior angle = $\frac{360°}{n}$

So n = $\frac{360°}{\text{exterior angle}}$

n = $\frac{360°}{30°}$ = 12

QUICK TEST

1. Find the sizes of the angles below labelled by letters.

a)
b)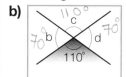
c)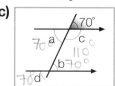

2. Find the size of an a) exterior and b) interior angle of a regular pentagon.

1. a) a = 150° b) b = 70°, c = 110°, d = 70°
c) a = 50°, b = 50°, c = 50°, d = 130° 2. a) 72° b) 108°

BEARINGS

- A bearing is the direction travelled between two points, given as an angle in degrees.
- All bearings are measured clockwise from the north line.
- All bearings should be given as 3 figures, e.g. 225°, 043°, 006°.

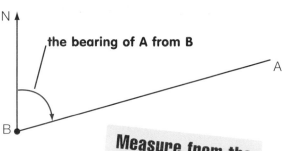

the bearing of A from B

Measure from the North Line at Q

EXAMPLES

Bearing of P
from Q = 060°

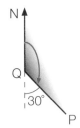

Bearing of P from Q =
180° – 30° = 150°

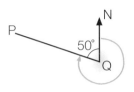

Bearing of P from Q
360° – 50° = 310°

BACK BEARINGS

When finding the back bearing (the bearing of Q from P above):
- draw in a north line at P;
- the two north lines are parallel lines, so the angle properties of parallel lines can be used.

Measure from the north line at P

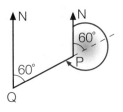

Bearing of Q from P
= 60° + 180° = 240°

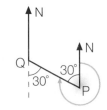

Bearing of Q from P
= 360° – 30° = 330°

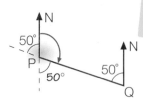

Bearing of Q from P =
180° – 50° = 130°

SCALE DRAWINGS AND BEARINGS

Scale drawings are useful for finding lengths and angles.

EXAMPLE

A ship sails from a harbour for 15 km on a bearing of 040°, and then continues due east for 20 km. Make a scale drawing of this journey using a scale of 1 cm to 5 km. How far will the ship have to sail to get back to the harbour by the shortest route? What will the bearing be?

Shortest route = 6.4 x 5 km = 32 km
Bearing = 70° + 180° = 250°

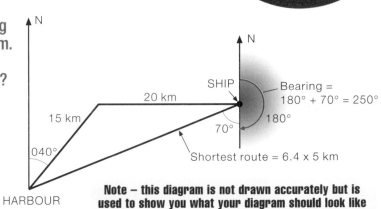

Note – this diagram is not drawn accurately but is used to show you what your diagram should look like

SCALES AND MAPS

A scale of 1 : 25000 means that 1 cm on the scale drawing represents a real length of 25000 cm.

Scales are often used on maps. They are usually written as a ratio.

EXAMPLE

The scale on a road map is 1 : 25000. Bury and Oldham are 20 cm apart on the map.
Work out the real distance, in km, between Bury and Oldham.
Scale 1 : 25000, distance on map is 20 cm.
   Real distance = 20 x 25000 = 500000 cm
Divide by 100 to change cm to m.
   500000 / 100 = 5000 m
Divide by 1000 to change m to km.
   5000 / 1000 = 5 km

BEARINGS AND SCALE DRAWINGS

QUICK TEST

1. What are the bearings of A from B in the following:

a)

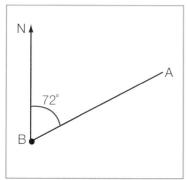

b)

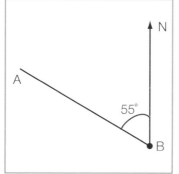

c)

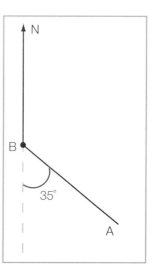

2. For each of the questions above work out the bearing of B from A.

3. The scale on a road map is 1 : 50000. If two towns are 14 cm apart on the map, work out the real distance between them.

TRANSLATIONS

These move figures from one place to another. The size and shape of the figure are not changed.
Vectors are used to describe the distance and direction of the translation.
A vector is written $\begin{bmatrix} a \\ b \end{bmatrix}$. $\underline{a}$ represents the horizontal movement, and $\underline{b}$ represents the vertical movement.

EXAMPLE

a) Translate ABC by the vector $\begin{bmatrix} 2 \\ 1 \end{bmatrix}$.
   Call it P.

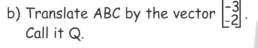

This means 2 to the right and 1 upwards.

b) Translate ABC by the vector $\begin{bmatrix} -3 \\ -2 \end{bmatrix}$.
   Call it Q.

This means 3 to the left and 2 down.

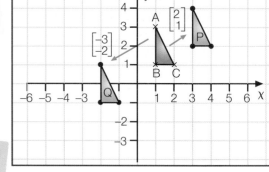

P and Q are congruent.
Remember that two shapes are congruent if one is exactly the same as the other.

TRANSFORMATIONS ①

REFLECTIONS

These create an image of an object on the other side of the mirror line. The mirror line is known as an axis of reflection. The size and shape of the figure are not changed.

EXAMPLE

Reflect triangle ABC in:
a) the X axis, and call it D;
b) the line y = –X, and call it E;
c) the line X = 5, and call it F.
D, E and F are congruent to triangle ABC.

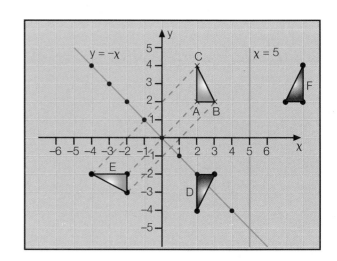

Count the squares of the object from the mirror; it's easier.

ROTATIONS

These **turn** a figure through an angle about some fixed point. This fixed point is called the **centre of rotation**. The size and shape of the figure are not changed.

EXAMPLE

Rotate triangle ABC:
a) 90° clockwise about (0, 0) and call it R;
b) 180° about (0, 0), and call it S;
c) 90° anticlockwise about (–1, –1), and call it T.

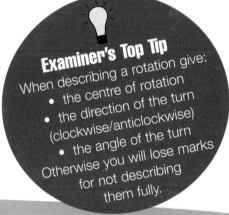

Examiner's Top Tip
When describing a rotation give:
• the centre of rotation
• the direction of the turn (clockwise/anticlockwise)
• the angle of the turn
Otherwise you will lose marks for not describing them fully.

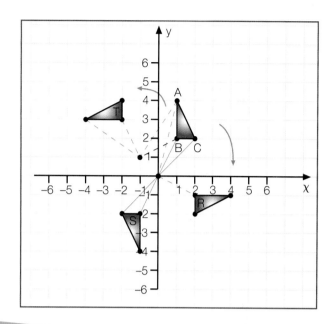

A **transformation** changes the **position** or **size** of a shape. There are four types of transformations: translations, reflections, rotations and enlargements.

QUICK TEST

1. On the diagram below:

a) Translate ABC by the vector $\begin{bmatrix} -3 \\ 1 \end{bmatrix}$
   Call it P

b) Reflect ABC in the line y = x. Call it Q

c) Reflect ABC in the line y = –1. Call it R

d) Rotate ABC 180° about (0, 0). Call it S

2. What does the vector $\begin{bmatrix} -2 \\ 3 \end{bmatrix}$ mean?

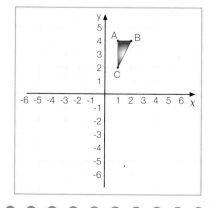

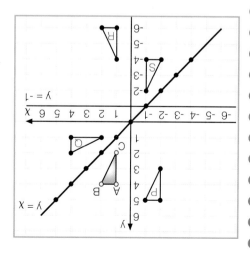

ENLARGEMENTS

These change the size but not the shape of an object.
The <u>centre</u> <u>of</u> <u>enlargement</u> is the point from which the enlargement takes place. The <u>scale</u> <u>factor</u> indicates how many times the lengths of the original figure have changed size.
• If the scale factor is <u>greater</u> <u>than</u> <u>1</u>, the shape becomes <u>bigger</u>.
• If the scale factor is <u>less</u> <u>than</u> <u>1</u>, the shape becomes <u>smaller</u>.

EXAMPLE
Enlarge triangle ABC by a scale factor of 2,
centre = (0, 0). Call it A'B'C'.

Notice each side of the enlargement is twice the size of the original.
A'B' = 2AB

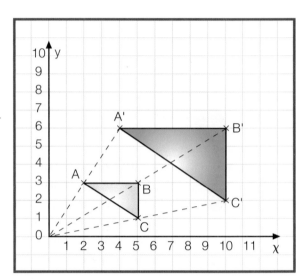

TRANSFORMATIONS ②

EXAMPLE
Describe fully the transformation that maps ABCDEF onto A'B'C'D'E'F'.
• To find the centre of enlargement, join A to A', and continue the line. Join B to B', and continue the line. Do the same for the others.
• Where all the lines meet is the centre of enlargement (–1, 3).
• The transformation is an enlargement with scale factor $\frac{1}{3}$. The centre of enlargement is at (–1, 3).

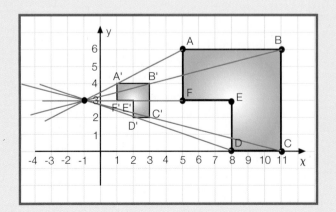

COMBINING TRANSFORMATIONS

These are a series of two or more transformations.

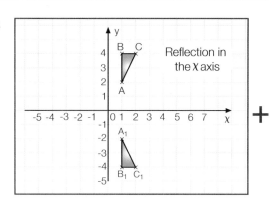

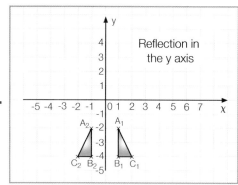

+

EXAMPLE

For triangle ABC:

a) Reflect ABC in the x axis. Call the image $A_1B_1C_1$.

b) Reflect $A_1B_1C_1$ in the y axis. Call the image $A_2B_2C_2$.

The single transformation that maps ABC onto $A_2B_2C_2$ directly is a rotation of 180°, centre (0, 0).

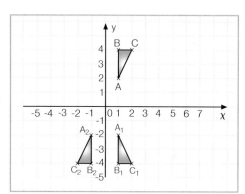

Examiner's Top Tip
When asked to describe an enlargement, you must include the scale factor and the position of the centre of enlargement.

- -

QUICK TEST

1. **Draw an enlargement of shape P with a scale factor of 2, centre of enlargement as shown.**

2. **a) Rotate the shaded shape through a 90° clockwise rotation about (0, 0). Call this shape B.**

   b) Reflect shape B in the x axis and call this shape C.

1.

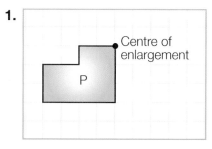

Centre of enlargement

P

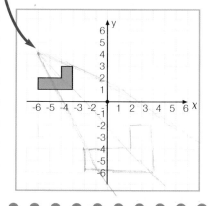

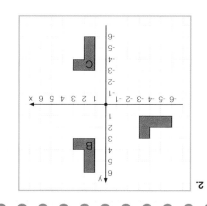

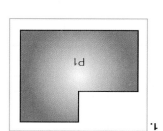

2.

1.

SIMILARITY

SIMILAR SHAPES

Similar figures are those which are the **same** **shape** but **different** **sizes**.
Corresponding angles are equal.
Corresponding lengths are in the same ratio.

Corresponding angles are equal.

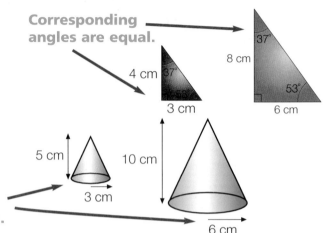

EXAMPLES
Notice corresponding lengths are in the same ratio. The lengths of the bigger cone are twice the size of the smaller cone.

FINDING MISSING LENGTHS OF SIMILAR FIGURES

EXAMPLE
Find the missing length a, giving your answer to 2 s.f.

$\frac{a}{11} = \frac{9}{14}$ Corresponding sides are in the same ratio.

$a = \frac{9}{14} \times 11$ Multiply both sides by 11.

$a = 7.1$ cm (2 s.f.)

9 cm   14 cm
a   11 cm

It is useful to draw the two triangles first.

EXAMPLE
Calculate the missing length.

$\frac{x}{6} = \frac{24}{16}$ Corresponding sides are in the same ratio.

$x = \frac{24}{16} \times 6$ Multiply both sides by 6.

$x = 9$ cm

Measurements in cm

Examiner's Top Tip
Always make sure you put the corresponding sides in the correct order and remember that whatever you are trying to work out must go on the top of the fraction otherwise you will have a tricky calculation to do.

QUICK TEST

1. Find the lengths labelled by the letters in these similar shapes

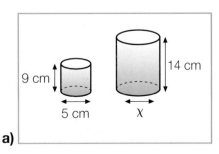

a)

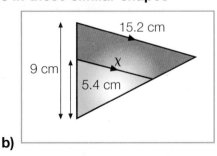

b)

LOCI AND COORDINATES IN 3D

The locus of a point is the set of all the possible positions which that point can occupy, subject to some given condition or rule.
The plural of locus is loci.

COMMON LOCI

- The locus of the points which are a constant distance from a fixed point is a circle. (i)
- The locus of the points which are equidistant from two points XY is the perpendicular bisector of XY. (ii)
- The locus of the points which are equidistant from two lines is the line which bisects the angle. (iii)
- The locus of the points which are a constant distance from a line XY is a pair of parallel lines above and below XY. (iv)

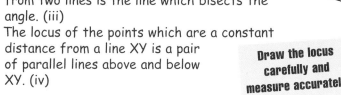

(i) Locus • P

(ii) Perpendicular bisector — X Y

(iii) Locus

(iv) X———Y

> Draw the locus carefully and measure accurately.

EXAMPLE
A new hospital (H) is being built so that it is equidistant from the train station and the gas depot. The hospital cannot be within 80 m of the gas depot in case of a leak. Using a scale of 1 cm to 20 m, show the first available position for where the hospital can be built.
- Construct the perpendicular bisector between the train station and the gas depot.
- Draw a circle of radius 4 cm since nothing can be built within 80 m of the depot.
- The hospital (H) is shown.

> Note – this is not drawn to scale but is used to show you what your diagram should look like.

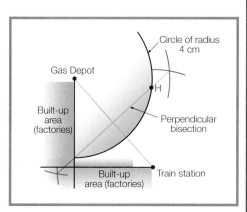

Circle of radius 4 cm
Gas Depot
H
Built-up area (factories)
Perpendicular bisection
Built-up area (factories)
Train station

COORDINATES IN 3D

This involves the extension of the normal x – y coordinates into a third direction, known as z. All positions then have three coordinates (x, y, z).

EXAMPLE
For the cuboid the vertices would have the following coordinates:
A (3, 0, 0)
B (3, 2, 0)
C (0, 2, 0)
D (0, 2, 1)
E (0, 0, 1)
F (3, 0, 1)
G (3, 2, 1)
O (0, 0, 0)

3 cm   1 cm   2 cm

> **Examiner's Top Tip**
> When answering loci questions use the construction techniques previously shown: this will ensure your work is accurate.

QUICK TEST

A gold coin is buried in the rectangular field. It is:

a) 4 m from T

b) Equidistant from RU and RS
   Mark with an X the position
   of the gold coin

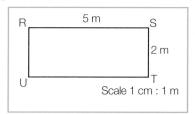

R ——5 m—— S
2 m
U ——— T
Scale 1 cm : 1 m

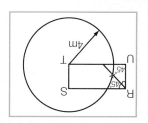

FINDING THE LENGTH OF THE HYPOTENUSE

Remember: Pythagoras' theorem can only be used for right-angled triangles.

Step 1 Square the two numbers that you are given.

Step 2 To find the hypotenuse (longest side) **add** these two squared numbers.

Step 3 After adding the two lengths find the square root of your answer.

EXAMPLE
Find the length of AB, giving your answer to 1 decimal place.
Using Pythagoras' theorem gives:

$AB^2 = AC^2 + BC^2$
$= 12^2 + 14.5^2$
$= 354.25$
$AB = \sqrt{354.25}$ Square root to find AB.
$= 18.8m$ (to 1 d.p.)   Round to 1 d.p.

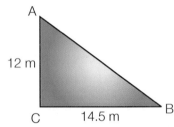

PYTHAGORAS' THEOREM

THE HYPOTENUSE IS THE LONGEST SIDE OF A RIGHT-ANGLED TRIANGLE.
IT IS ALWAYS OPPOSITE THE RIGHT ANGLE.

SOLVING PROBLEMS

EXAMPLE
· Calculate the height of this isosceles triangle.

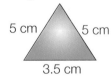

5 cm   5 cm

3.5 cm

· Split the triangle down the middle to make it right-angled.
Using Pythagoras' theorem gives:

$5^2 = h^2 + 1.75^2$
$h^2 = 5^2 - 1.75^2$
$h^2 = 21.9375$
$h^2 = \sqrt{21.9375} = 4.68$ cm (to 2 d.p.)

5 cm   h

1.75 cm

EXAMPLE
· A ladder of length 13 m rests against a wall.
The height up the wall the ladder reaches is 12 m.
How far away from the wall is the foot of the ladder?

$13^2 = x^2 + 12^2$
$13^2 - 12^2 = x^2$
$169 - 144 = x^2$
$x^2 = 25$
$x = \sqrt{25} = 5$ m

The foot of the ladder is 5 m away from the wall.

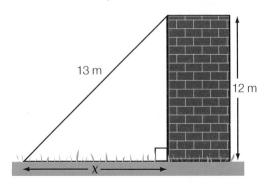

13 m

12 m

x

FINDING THE LENGTH OF A SHORTER SIDE

Follow the steps for finding the hypotenuse except:
Step 2 to find the shorter length subtract the smaller value from the larger value.
• Remember to square root ($\sqrt{\ }$) your answer.

EXAMPLE

Find the length of FG, leaving your answer in surd form.
Using Pythagoras' theorem gives:

$EF^2 = EG^2 + FG^2$
$FG^2 = EF^2 - EG^2$
$\quad\ = 9^2 - 8^2$
$\quad\ = 17$
$FG\ = \sqrt{17}$

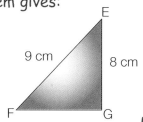

leaving an answer in surd form just means to leave it with a square root

Rearrange the formula:
use $a^2 = c^2 - b^2$

Examiner's Top Tip

Pythagoras' theorem allows us to calculate the length of one of the sides of a right-angled triangle, when the other two sides are known. If you are not told to what degree of accuracy to round your answer be guided by significant figures given in the question.

Pythagoras' theorem states:
in any right-angled triangle,
the square on the hypotenuse
is equal to the sum of the
squares on the other two
sides.
Using the letters in the
diagram, the theorem
is written as:

$c^2 = a^2 + b^2$

This may be rearranged
to give $a^2 = c^2 - b^2$ or
$b^2 = c^2 - a^2$, which are useful
when calculating
one of the shorter sides.

CALCULATING THE LENGTH OF A LINE AB, GIVEN TWO SETS OF COORDINATES

By drawing in a triangle between
the two points A (1, 2) and B (7, 6)
we can find the length of AB by
Pythagoras' Theorem.

Horizontal distance = 6 (7 – 1)
Vertical distance = 4 (6 – 2)
Length of $(AB)^2 = 6^2 + 4^2$
$\quad\quad\ (AB)^2 = 36 + 16$
$\quad\quad\ (AB)^2 = 52$
$\quad\quad\quad\ AB = \sqrt{52}$
Length of AB = 7.21

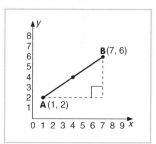

The midpoint of AB,
M has coordinates (4, 4)
i.e. $\dfrac{(1 + 7)}{2}, \dfrac{2 + 6}{2}$

QUICK TEST

1. Calculate the lengths of the
   sides marked with a letter.
   Give your answers to 1 d.p.

a)
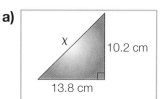
10.2 cm
13.8 cm
x

b)
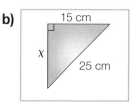
15 cm
25 cm
x

2. Work out the length of the diagonal
   on this rectangle.

2.
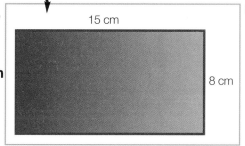
15 cm
8 cm

3. A ship sets off from Port A
   and travels 50 km North then
   80 km East to reach Port B.
   How far is Port A from Port
   B by the shortest route?

3.
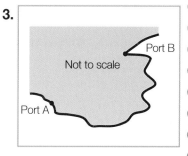
Port B
Not to scale
Port A

LABELLING THE SIDES OF THE TRIANGLE

<u>hyp</u> (hypotenuse) is opposite the right angle.
<u>opp</u> (opposite side) is opposite the angle θ.
<u>adj</u> (adjacent side) is next to the angle θ.

θ is a Greek letter called <u>theta</u> and is used to represent <u>angles</u>.

Opposite (opp)   Hypotenuse (hyp)

θ

(adj) Adjacent

TRIGONOMETRY IN RIGHT-ANGLED TRIANGLES

Trigonometry in right-angled triangles can be used to calculate an unknown angle or an unknown length.

CALCULATING THE SIZE OF AN ANGLE

EXAMPLE
Calculate angle $\hat{ABC}$.

$\tan \theta = \dfrac{opp}{adj}$ Label the sides and decide on the ratio.

$\tan \theta = \dfrac{15}{27}$ Divide the top value by the bottom value.

$\tan \theta = 0.\dot{5}$

$\theta = 29.1°$ (1 d.p.)

> To find the angle you usually use the second function on your calculator.

On the calculator type in

| 15 | ÷ | 27 | = | inv | tan | = |

You may have a shift key on your calculator.

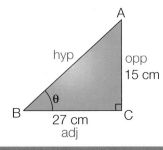

Examiner's Top Tip
Note – check your calculator as you may have to do it differently.

TRIGONOMETRIC RATIOS

The three trigonometric ratios are:

$\text{Sin } \theta = \dfrac{\text{opposite}}{\text{hypotenuse}}$

$\text{Cos } \theta = \dfrac{\text{adjacent}}{\text{hypotenuse}}$

$\text{Tan } \theta = \dfrac{\text{opposite}}{\text{adjacent}}$

The made-up word

<u>SOH CAH TOA</u>

is a quick way of remembering the ratios. The word comes from the first letters of <u>S</u>in equals <u>O</u>pposite divided by <u>H</u>ypotenuse, etc.

To enter sin 30 into the calculator you usually do it backwards, i.e. **30 SIN** (although some calculators do it forwards: check yours!)

CALCULATING THE LENGTH OF A SIDE

EXAMPLE

Calculate the length of BC.
- Label the sides first.
- Decide on the ratio.
  $$\sin 30° = \frac{opp}{hyp}$$

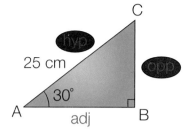

- Substitute in the values.
  $$\sin 30° = \frac{BC}{25}$$

  $25 \times \sin 30° = BC$ Multiply both sides by 25.
  $BC = 12.5$ cm

Examiner's Top Tip
When calculating the size of an angle it should usually be rounded to 1 d.p. However do not round off your answer until right at the end of the question. You must learn the trigonometric ratios as they are no longer on the formula sheets.

EXAMPLE

Calculate the length of EF.
$$\cos 40° = \frac{adj}{hyp} = \frac{20}{EF}$$

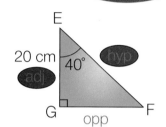

$EF \times \cos 40° = 20$ Multiply both sides by EF.
$EF = \dfrac{20}{\cos 40°}$ Divide both sides by cos 40°.

   $= 26.1$ cm (1 d.p.)

| 20 | ÷ | 40 | cos | = | or | 20 | ÷ | cos | 40 | = |

QUICK TEST

1. Label the sides of these triangles with respect to θ.

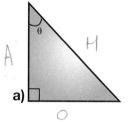 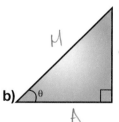 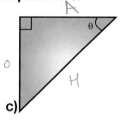

a)   b)   c)

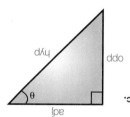

c.

2. Calculate the length of X in each triangle.

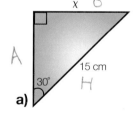 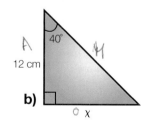 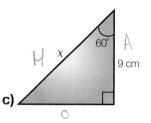

a)   b)   c)

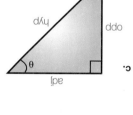

b.

3. Work out the size of the angle in each of these triangles.

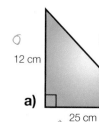 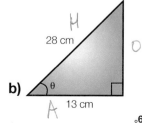 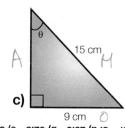

a)   b)   c)

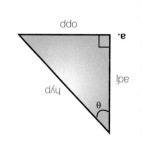

a.

1. (see below)   2. a) 7.5 cm   b) 10.1 cm   c) 18 cm   3. a) 25.6°   b) 62.3°   c) 36.9°

GCSE SAMPLE QUESTION

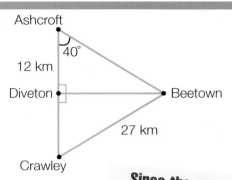

The diagram shows the position
of four towns.
Beetown is due east of Diveton.
Crawley is 27 km from Beetown.
Ashcroft is 12 km due north of Diveton.
Beetown is on a bearing of 140° from Ashcroft.

a) Calculate the distance from Diveton to Beetown.
Give your answer in kilometres correct to 1 d.p.

$\tan 40° = \dfrac{\text{opp}}{\text{adj}}$ ✓ $\tan 40° = \dfrac{X}{12}$

$12 \times \tan 40° = X$ ✓
$X = 10.1$ km
10.1 km ✓

Since the opposite and adjacent sides are used the tangent ratio is needed.

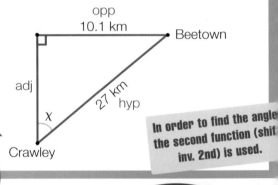

b) Calculate the bearing of Beetown from Crawley,
giving your answer to the nearest degree.

$\sin X = \dfrac{\text{opp}}{\text{hyp}}$ $\sin X = \dfrac{10.1}{27}$

$\sin X = 0.374074$
$X = 21.97$ ✓
Bearing = 022°

Do not round off until the end of the question.

In order to find the angle the second function (shift inv. 2nd) is used.

APPLICATION OF TRIGONOMETRY

Examiner's Top Tip
Check that you know how to use your calculator for trigonometry questions. It is helpful to draw the individual triangle that you are using – this will allow you to label it properly.

ANGLES OF ELEVATION AND DEPRESSION

*The **angle of elevation** is measured from the horizontal **upwards**.*

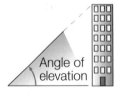

Angle of elevation

*The **angle of depression** is measured from the horizontal **downwards**.*

Angle of depression

QUICK TEST

Dipak stands 30 m from the base of a tower. He
measures the angle of elevation from ground level
to the top of the tower as 50°. Calculate the height
of the tower. Give your answer to 3 s.f.

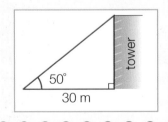

35.8 m (3 s.f.)

ANGLE PROPERTIES OF CIRCLES

CIRCLE THEOREMS

There are several theorems you need to know and be able to apply. The theorems are:

1. The perpendicular bisector of any chord passes through the centre.

2. The angle in a semicircle is always 90°.

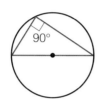

3. The radius and a tangent always meet at 90°.

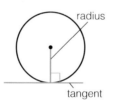

4. Angles in the same segment are equal, e.g. ABĈC = ADĈC

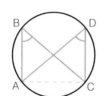

5. The angle at the centre is twice the angle at the circumference, e.g. PÔQ = 2 x PR̂Q

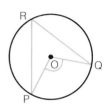

6. Opposite angles of a cyclic quadrilateral add up to 180°.
(A cyclic quadrilateral is a 4-sided shape with each corner touching the circle), i.e.   χ + y = 180°
         a + b = 180°

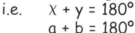
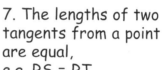

7. The lengths of two tangents from a point are equal, e.g. RS = RT

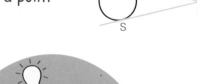

EXAM STYLE QUESTION

Calculate the angles marked with letters a – d in the diagram below

a = 140° (2 x angle at circumference)
b = ½(180° – 140°) (angles in an isosceles triangle)
   = 40° ÷ 2
   = 20°
c = 90° – 20°
(radius and tangent meet at 90°)
   = 70°
d = 180° – (2 x 70°)
(angles in an isosceles triangle PQR)
   = 40°

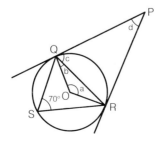

QUICK TEST

Calculate the missing angles in the diagram below.

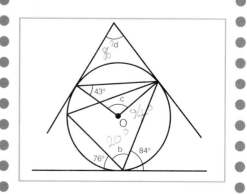

b = 20° c = 94° d = 86°

METRIC UNITS

Length	Weight	Capacity
10 mm = 1 cm	1000 mg = 1 g	1000 ml = 1 l
100 cm = 1 m	1000 g = 1 kg	100 cl = 1 l
1000 m = 1 km	1000 kg = 1 tonne	1000 cm³ = 1 l

CONVERTING UNITS

- If changing from <u>small</u> units to <u>large</u> units (for example, g to kg), <u>divide</u>.
- If changing from <u>large</u> units to <u>small</u> units (for example, km to m), <u>multiply</u>.

EXAMPLES

(a) Change 50 mm into cm.
mm are smaller than cm, so divide by the number of mm in a cm.
50 ÷ 10 = 5 cm.

(b) Change 6 km into mm.
km are bigger than mm, so multiply by the number of m in a km,
cm in a m and mm in a cm.
6 x 1000 x 100 x 10 = 6 000 000 mm.

km → m → cm → mm
x 1000   x 100   x 10

COMPOUND MEASURES

Speed can be measured in kilometres per hour (km/h), miles per hour (m.p.h.) and metres per second (m/s). km/h, m.p.h. and m/s are all <u>compound measures</u> because they involve a combination of basic measures.

SPEED

average speed = $\dfrac{\text{total distance travelled}}{\text{total time taken}}$

$$s = \dfrac{d}{t}$$

Always check the units first, before starting a question. Change them if necessary.

EXAMPLE

A car travels 50 miles in 1 hour 20 minutes. Find the speed in miles per hour.
Change the time units first:
20 minutes = $\frac{20}{60}$ of 1 hour
$s = \dfrac{d}{t} = \dfrac{50}{1\frac{20}{60}} = 37.5$ m.p.h.

From the speed formula two other formulae can be found.

time = $\dfrac{\text{distance}}{\text{speed}}$ distance = speed x time

$s = \dfrac{d}{t}$ $t = \dfrac{d}{s}$ $d = st$

Just remember the letters. It's quicker.

EXAMPLE

A car travels a distance of 240 miles at an average speed of 65 m.p.h. How long does it take?
time = $\dfrac{\text{distance}}{\text{speed}}$ so $t = \dfrac{240}{65} = 3.692$ hours

3.692 hours must be changed to hours and minutes.
- Subtract the hours. So 3.692 – 3 = 0.692
- Multiply the decimal part by 60 minutes.
0.692 x 60 = 42 minutes (nearest minute)
- Time = 3 hours 42 minutes.

DENSITY

density = $\dfrac{\text{mass}}{\text{volume}}$ volume = $\dfrac{\text{mass}}{\text{density}}$

mass = density x volume

$D = \dfrac{M}{V}$ $V = \dfrac{M}{D}$ $M = DV$

EXAMPLE

Find the density of an object whose mass is 400 g and whose volume is 25 cm³
density = $\dfrac{M}{V} = = 16$ g/cm³

Since the mass is in grams, volume is in cm³. Density is in g/cm³.

IMPERIAL UNITS

Length	Weight	Capacity
1 foot = **12 inches**	**1 stone =** **14 pounds (lb)**	**20 fluid oz =** **1 pint**
1 yard = **3 feet**	**1 pound =** **16 ounces (oz)**	**8 pints =** **1 gallon**

EXAMPLES

a) Change 4 yards into inches.
Change yards to feet (x 3) and feet to inches (x 12).
4 x 3 x 12 = 144 inches.

b) Change 166 pints into gallons.
8 pints = 1 gallon, so 1 pint = $\frac{1}{8}$ gallon.
166 ÷ 8 = 20.75 gallons.

COMPARISONS BETWEEN METRIC AND IMPERIAL UNITS

Length	Weight	Capacity
*2.5 cm ≈ 1 inch	*25 g ≈ 1 ounce	*1 litre ≈ 1$\frac{3}{4}$ pints
*30 cm ≈ 1 foot	*1 kg ≈ 2.2 pounds	*4.5 litres ≈ 1 gallon
*1 m ≈ 39 inches		
*8 km ≈ 5 miles		

*All of the comparisons between metric and imperial units are only approximate.

EXAMPLE

Change 25 km into miles.
8 km ≈ 5 miles.
1 km ≈ $\frac{5}{8}$ mile = 0.625 miles.
25 km ≈ 25 x 0.625 = 15.625 miles.

Examiner's Top Tip
There is a lot of learning to do in this section. Try and learn all the
- metric and imperial conversions
- formulas for speed, distance and time. Use the formula triangle to help you.

$\dfrac{D}{S \times T}$

MEASURES AND MEASUREMENT

ACCURACY OF MEASUREMENT

There are two types of measurements: discrete measurements and continous measurements.

DISCRETE MEASURES
These are quantities that can be counted; for example, the number of baked bean tins on a shelf.

CONTINUOUS MEASURES
These are measurements which have been made by using a measuring instrument; for example, the height of a person. Continuous measures are <u>not exact</u>.

EXAMPLE
Nigel weighs 72 kg to the nearest kg. His actual weight could be anywhere between 71.5 kg and 72.5 kg.

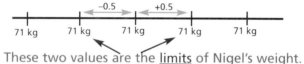

These two values are the <u>limits</u> of Nigel's weight.

If W represents weight, then

$$71.5 \le W < 72.5$$

This is the <u>lower</u> <u>limit</u> of Nigel's weight (sometimes known as the <u>lower</u> <u>bound</u>). Anything below 71.5 would be recorded as 71 kg.

This is the <u>upper</u> <u>limit</u> (<u>upper</u> <u>bound</u>) of Nigel's weight. Anything from 72.5 upwards would be recorded as 73 kg.

> In general, if a measurement is accurate to some given amount, then the true value lies within a maximum of a half a unit of that amount.

EXAMPLE
The length of a seedling is measured as 3.7 cm to the nearest tenth of a cm. What are the upper and lower limits of the length?

```
         −0.05      +0.05
   ├──────┼──────┼──────┼──────┤
  3.6    3.65    3.7    3.75   3.8
lower limit      3.65 ≤ L < 3.75      upper limit
```

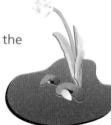

QUICK TEST

1. Change 3500 g into kg. *3.5 kg*

2. Change 3 kg into pounds.

3. Change 6 litres into pints.

4. Write down the upper and lower limits for a time of 9.2 seconds, rounded to the nearest tenth of a second.

5. Write down the upper and lower limits for a weight of 58 kg, rounded to the nearest kg.

6. Amy walks 6 miles in 2 hours 40 minutes. Find her average speed.

7. Find the time taken for a car to travel 600 miles at an average speed of 70 m.p.h.

8. Find the density of an object whose mass is 20 g and whose volume is 9 cm³.

1. 3.5 kg   2. 6.6 lb   3. 10½ pints   4. 9.15 ≤ 9.2 < 9.25   5. 57.5 ≤ 58 < 58.5   6. 2.25 m.p.h.   7. 8.57 hours (or 8 hours 34 minutes)   8. 2.2 g/cm³

AREAS OF QUADRILATERALS AND TRIANGLES

AREA OF A RECTANGLE
Area = length x width
A = l x w

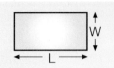

AREA OF A PARALLELOGRAM
Area = base x perpendicular height
Remember to use the perpendicular height, not the slant height.
A = b x h

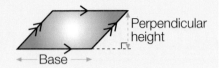

AREA OF A TRIANGLE
Area = $\frac{1}{2}$ base x perpendicular height
A = $\frac{1}{2}$ x b x h

AREA OF A TRAPEZIUM
Area = $\frac{1}{2}$ x (sum of parallel sides) x perpendicular height between them
A = $\frac{1}{2}$ x (a + b) x h

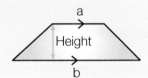

EXAMPLES
Find the areas of the following shapes, giving the answers to 3 s.f. where necessary.

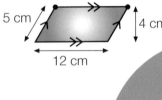

a) A = b x h
 = 12 x 4
 = 48 cm²

b) A = $\frac{1}{2}$ x (a + b) x h
 = $\frac{1}{2}$ x (4.9 + 10.1) x 6.2
 = 46.5 cm²

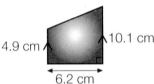

Examiner's Top Tip
You have got lots more formulae to learn here. You need to know all these formulae (except the trapezium), otherwise you will find answering the questions very difficult.

EXAMPLE
If the area of this triangle is 55 cm², find the height, giving your answer to 3 s.f.

A = $\frac{1}{2}$ x b x h   Substitute the values into
55 = 1/2 x 16.9 x h   the formula.
55 = 8.45 x h   Divide both sides by 8.45.
$\frac{55}{8.45}$ = h   So h = 6.51 cm (to 3 s.f.)

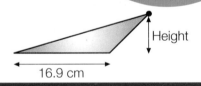

AREAS OF ENLARGEMENTS AND CHANGING AREA UNITS

This usually catches everybody out. If a shape is enlarged by a scale factor n then:
The AREA is n^2 times bigger.

EXAMPLE
If n = 2:
● the lengths are twice as big
● the area is 4 times as big (n^2 = 4).

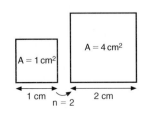

EXAMPLE
The square has a length of 1 metre.

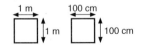

This is the same as a length of 100 cm.
Area = 1 m² Area = 10 000 cm²
Therefore 1 m² = 10 000 cm² (not 100 as most people think!)
Because of this possible mistake it's always better to change the units before you start a question.

CIRCUMFERENCE AND AREA OF A CIRCLE

circumference	= π x diameter = 2 x π x radius	C = π x d = 2 x π x r
area	= π x (radius)²	A = π x r²

EXAMPLE

The diameter of a circular rose garden is 5 m.
Find the circumference and area of the rose garden.

C = π x d   Substitute in the formula.

= 3.14 x 5   Use π ÷ 3.14 or
                  the value of π on
                  your calculator.

= 15.7 m   EXP often gives the
                  value of π.

5 m

When finding the area, work out the radius first.
d = 2 x r so r = d ÷ 2, and r = 2.5 m

A = π x r²

= 3.14 x 2.5²   Remember 2.5² means 2.5 x 2.5.

= 19.625

= 19.6 m² (3 s.f.)

Note – this answer could be left as 6.25π, i.e. in terms of π.

EXAMPLE

A circle has an area of 40 cm². Find the radius of
the circle, giving your answer to 3 s.f. Use π = 3.14.

A = π x r²

40 = 3.14 x r²   Substitute the values into
                        the formula.

$\frac{40}{3.14}$ = r²   Divide both sides by 3.14.

r² = 12.738 . . .

r = √12.738 . . .Take the square root to find r.

= 3.57 cm (3 s.f.)

Remember r² means r X r

AREA OF 2D SHAPES

PERIMETER AND AREA OF 2D SHAPES

Perimeter: this is the distance around the outside edge of a shape.

Area: this is the amount of space a 2D shape covers.

Common units of area are mm², cm², m², etc.

QUICK TEST

Work out the areas of the following shapes, giving your answers to 3 s.f.

1. a)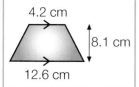
4.2 cm
8.1 cm
12.6 cm

b)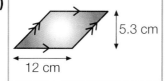
5.3 cm
12 cm

c)
9 cm

d)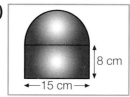
8 cm
15 cm

2. Work out the area
   of the shaded region.

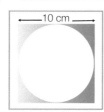
10 cm

VOLUME OF PRISMS

A prism is any solid which can be cut into slices, which are all the same shape. This is called having a uniform cross-section.

VOLUME OF A CUBOID
volume =
length x width x height
V = l x w x h

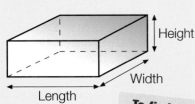

Height
Width
Length

VOLUME OF A PRISM
volume = area of
cross-section x length
V = a x l

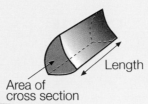

Length
Area of cross section

VOLUME OF A CYLINDER
Cylinders are prisms where the cross-section is a circle.
volume = area of cross-section x length

Radius

$$V = \pi r^2 \text{ x h}$$

area of circle   height or length

Height

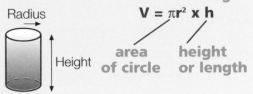

To find the surface area of a cuboid work out the area of each face and then add them together.
SA = 2lh + 2wh + 2lw.

EXAMPLES
Find the volumes of the following 3D shapes, giving the answer to 3 s.f. Use π = 3.14.

The area of cross-section is the area of a triangle.

a) V = a x l
$= (\frac{1}{2} \text{ x b x h}) \text{ x l}$
$= (\frac{1}{2} \text{ x 9.6 x 7}) \text{ x 15.1}$
= 507.36 cm³
= 507 cm³ (3 s.f.)

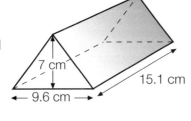

7 cm
9.6 cm
15.1 cm

b) V = πr^2 x h
= 3.14 x 10.7² x 24.1
= 8663.92 cm³
= 8660 cm³ (3 s.f.)

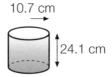

10.7 cm
24.1 cm

EXAMPLE
If the volume of the cylinder is 500 cm³, work out the radius. (Use π = 3.14.)

9.7 cm
r

V = πr^2 x h
500 = 3.14 x r² x 9.7   Substitute into the formula.

500 = 30.458 x r²

$\frac{500}{30.458} = r^2$ Divide both sides by 30.458.

r² = 16.416 . . .   Take the square root to find the radius.

r $\sqrt{16.416 \ldots}$ So r = 4.05 cm (3 s.f.)

VOLUMES OF ENLARGEMENTS

Just like areas these usually catch people out!
For an enlargement of scale factor n:
The volumes are n^3 times bigger.

EXAMPLE
If a cube of length 1 cm is enlarged by a scale factor of 2:
i.e. n = 2 so V = 2^3 = 8 times bigger

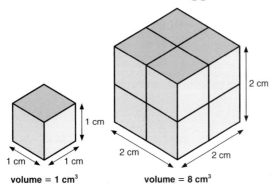

1 cm
1 cm   1 cm
volume = 1 cm³

2 cm
2 cm   2 cm
volume = 8 cm³

CONVERTING VOLUME UNITS

Another tricky topic which usually catches everybody out!

EXAMPLE
The cube has a length of 1 m – this is the same as a length of 100 cm.
Therefore 1 m³ = 1 000 000 cm³
not quite what you think!
It's probably better therefore to change all the lengths to the same unit before starting a question!

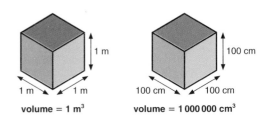

1 m
1 m   1 m
volume = 1 m³

100 cm
100 cm   100 cm
volume = 1 000 000 cm³

VOLUME OF 3D SHAPES

VOLUME: THIS IS THE AMOUNT OF SPACE A 3D SHAPE OCCUPIES. COMMON UNITS OF VOLUME ARE MM³, CM³, M³, ETC.

Examiner's Top Tip
For any volume question work out carefully, check that you show full working out and show each step in your working.

DIMENSIONS

- The dimension of <u>perimeter</u> is <u>length</u> (L); it is a measurement in one dimension.
- The dimension of <u>area</u> is <u>length</u> x <u>length</u> ($L \times L = L^2$); it is a measurement in two dimensions.
- The dimension of <u>volume</u> is <u>length</u> x <u>length</u> x <u>length</u> ($L \times L \times L = L^3$); it is a measurement in three dimensions.
- Values like 3, $\frac{4}{\pi}$, 6.2, etc. have no dimensions.

EXAMPLES

The letters a, b, c and d all represent lengths. For each expression, write down whether it represents a length, area or volume.

a) $a^2 + b^2$ = (length x length) + (length x length) = area
$$\underline{L}^2 + \underline{L}^2$$

b) $\frac{1}{3} \pi \, abc$ = number x length x length x length = volume
$$\underline{L}^3$$

c) $2\pi a + \frac{3}{4}\pi d$ = (number x length) + (number x length) = length
$$\underline{L} + \underline{L}$$

d) $\frac{5}{9}\pi a^2 d + \pi b^2 c^2$ = (number x length x length x length) + (number x length² x length²) = none
$$\underline{L}^3 + \underline{L}^4$$

> A formula with a mixed dimension is impossible.

> A dimension greater than 3 is impossible, so it has no dimension.

QUICK TEST

1. Work out the volumes of the following 3D shapes. Give your answer to 3 s.f.

a)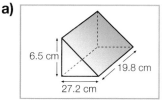

b)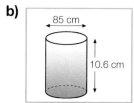

2. The volume of a cylinder is 2000 cm³ and the radius is 5.6 cm. Work out the height to 3 s.f.

3. x, y, z represent lengths. For each expression write down whether it could represent perimeter, area or volume.

   a) $\sqrt{x^2 + y^2 + z^2}$

   b) $\frac{5}{9}\pi x^3 + 2y^3$

   c) $\frac{1}{3} \frac{xyz^2}{y}$

   d) $\frac{9}{5}\pi xy + \frac{4}{5}\pi yz$

1. a) 1750 cm³ (3 s.f.) b) 60100 cm³ (3 s.f.)   2. 20.3 cm (3 s.f.)   3. a) Perimeter b) Volume c) Volume d) Area

EXAM QUESTIONS – Use the questions to test your progress. Check your answers on page 94.

1. a) Draw the lines of symmetry on the rectangle.
b) What is the order of rotational symmetry of the rectangle?

....

2. Calculate the sizes of the angles marked with letters.
a ....
b ....
c ....
d ....

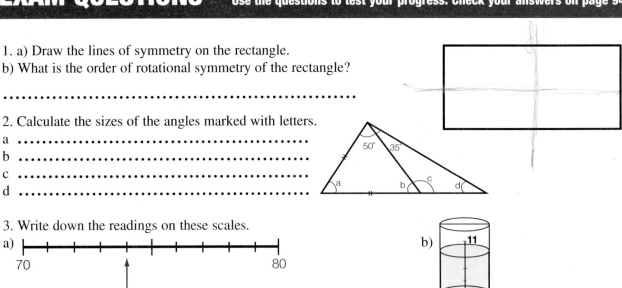

3. Write down the readings on these scales.
a)

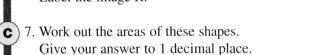

b)

4. Change 600 g into pounds.

....

c 5. The scale on a road map is 1 : 25000. Amersham and Watford are 30 cm apart on the map.
Work out the real distance in km between Amersham and Watford.

....

6. Draw the image of the shaded shape after an enlargement by
the scale factor $\frac{1}{2}$, with C as the centre of enlargement.
Label the image R.

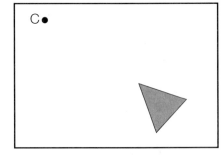

c 7. Work out the areas of these shapes.
Give your answer to 1 decimal place.
a)

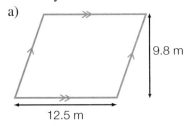

b)

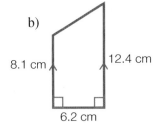

....

c 8. A car travels a distance of 320 miles at an average speed of 65 m.p.h. How long does it take?

....

c 9. A car travels 70 miles in 1 hour 20 minutes. Find the average speed in m.p.h.

....

10. Jerry said that, 'The distance between Manchester and London is 240 miles to the nearest
whole number.' Write down the smallest possible distance between Manchester and London.

....

c 11. A ladder of length 6 m rests so that the foot of the ladder is 3 m away from a wall.
Calculate how far up the wall the ladder reaches. Give your answer to 2 s.f.

....
....

c Indicates that a calculator may be used

c) 12. Calculate the volume of the oil drum, clearly stating your units.
Give your answer to three significant figures.

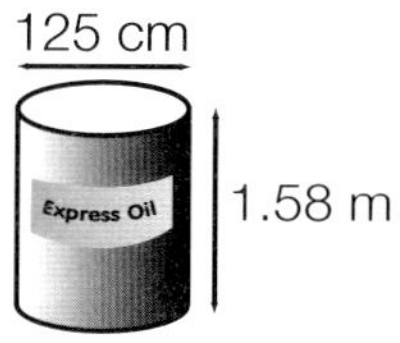

125 cm

Express Oil

1.58 m

....

....

....

c) 13. A ladder of length 12 m rests against a wall in such a way
that the angle which the ladder makes with the wall is 40°.
Calculate the height of the ladder above the ground,
giving your answer to 1 decimal place.

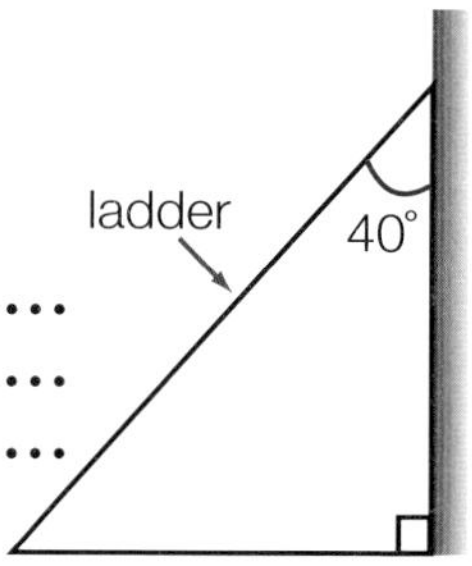

ladder   40°

....

....

....

c) 14. A ship sails due north for 200 km. It then sails due west for 140 km.
Calculate the bearing, to the nearest degree, of the ship from its starting point.

....

....

....

c) 15. In the diagram MN is parallel to YZ, YMX and ZNX
are straight lines, XM = 5.1 cm, XY = 9.5 cm, XN = 6.3 cm,
YZ = 6.8 cm. $\angle$YXZ = 29°, $\angle$XZY = 68°

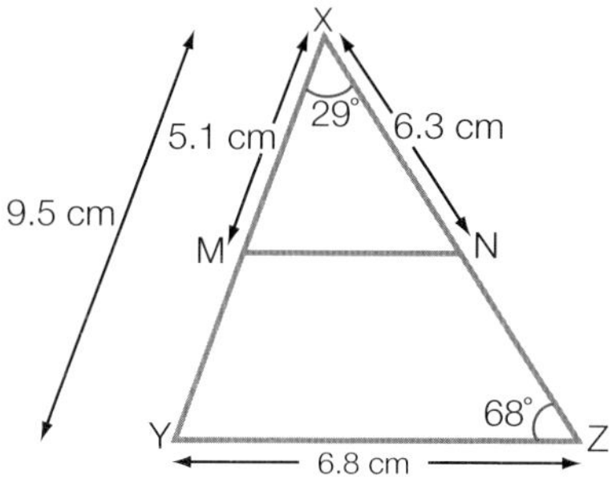

a) (i) Calculate the size of angle XMN ....

....

(ii) Explain how you obtained your answer ....

....

b) Calculate the length of MN ....

....

c) Calculate the length of XZ ....

....

X
29°
5.1 cm   6.3 cm
9.5 cm
M   N
Y   68° Z
6.8 cm

16. Here are some expressions:

$7r^2t$	$1\sqrt{r^2 + t^2}$	$\dfrac{rtl}{4}$	πr^2	$2\sqrt{r^2 + t^2}$	$2tl$	$4\dfrac{r^3}{t^2}$

The letters, r, t and l represent lengths. π, 2, 4 and 7 are numbers that have no dimensions.
Three of the expressions represent surface area. Tick the boxes (✓) underneath these three expressions.

How did you do?

1–5	correct	....start again
6–10	correct	....getting there
11–13	correct	....good work
14–16	correct	....excellent

TYPES OF DATA

There are two main types of data:

QUANTITATIVE
the answer is a number,
e.g. how many blue cars
in a car park?

QUALITATIVE
the answer is a word,
e.g. what is your
favourite colour?

QUANTITATIVE data can be discrete or continuous:

- **Discrete data:** has an exact value. Each category is separate and is usually found by counting. Examples include the number of people with brown hair.

- **Continuous data:** here the values change from one category to the next. Examples include the heights and weights of students. Continuous data cannot be measured exactly. The accuracy of the measurement relies on the accuracy of the measuring equipment.

- **Primary data:** this is data which is collected by the person who is going to analyse and use it.

- **Secondary data:** this is data which is available from an external source, such as books, newspapers and the internet.

COLLECTING DATA

The census is one of the largest surveys that takes place. The census is done every 10 years and its main aim is to give a 'snapshot' of Britain today. In order to carry out the census all households are given a survey to complete.

HYPOTHESES AND EXPERIMENTS

A hypothesis is a prediction which can be tested.
Experiments can be used to test hypotheses.

EXAMPLE

Hypothesis: The better the light, the faster seedlings grow.

Variable: This is the intensity of the light that can be changed.

Conditions: The other conditions must stay the same. All seedlings must be exactly the same size, strength and colour to start with. If there is bias (e.g. if one side of the tray gets extra sunlight), then the experiment needs to start again.

QUESTIONNAIRES

These can be used to test hypotheses.

WHEN DESIGNING QUESTIONNAIRES:
- ✔ Decide what needs to be found out: the hypothesis.
- ✔ Give instructions on how the questionnaire has to be filled in.
- ✔ Do not ask for information which is not needed (e.g. name).
- ✔ Make the questions clear and concise.
- ✔ Keep the questionnaire short.
- ✔ If people's opinions are needed, make sure the question is unbiased. An example of a biased question would be:
  'Do you agree that a leisure centre should have a tennis court rather than a squash court?'
- ✔ Allow for any possible answers, for example:
  Which of these is your favourite colour?

Examiner's Top Tip
When asked to design a questionnaire, always word the questions carefully. Try to avoid bias appearing in your questions.

Red	Blue	Green	Yellow	Other
☐	☐	☐	☐	☐

DATA COLLECTION SHEET

- When collecting data, a data collection sheet is often used.

EXAMPLE

Tracey and David carried out a survey on the colour of cars which passed the gates of their school during a 30-minute interval. The data collection sheet looked like this:

COLOUR OF CAR	TALLY	FREQUENCY

QUICK TEST

1. Richard and Tammy are carrying out a survey on some students' favourite foods. Design a data sheet that they could use.

2. Design a questionnaire you could give a friend in order to find out what they do in their spare time.

DRAWING PIE CHARTS

- These are used to illustrate data. They are circles split up into sections, each section representing a certain number of items.

EXAMPLE

The favourite sports of 24 students in year 11:

Sport	Frequency	Angle	Workings
Football	9	135°	$\frac{9}{24}$ x 360°
Swimming	5	75°	$\frac{5}{24}$ x 360°
Netball	3	45°	$\frac{3}{24}$ x 360°
Hockey	7	105°	$\frac{7}{24}$ x 360°
Total	24	360°	

To calculate the angles for the pie chart:
- Find the total for the items listed.
- Find the fraction of the total for each item.
- Multiply the fraction by 360° to find the angle.

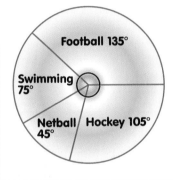

Key in on the calculator:
9 ÷ 24 X 360 =

INTERPRETING PIE CHARTS

EXAMPLE

The pie chart shows how some students travel to school.

There are 18 students in total.

How many travel by:

a) Car?

b) Bus?

c) Foot?

Bus 80°

Car 60°

Foot 220°

360° = 18 students

$1° = \frac{18}{360} = 0.05$ (work out 1°)

Car = 60° x 0.05 = 3 students

Bus = 80° x 0.05 = 4 students

Foot = 220° x 0.05 = 11 students

HISTOGRAMS

- These are drawn to illustrate continuous data. They are similar to bar charts except that there are no gaps between the bars. The data must be grouped into equal class intervals if the length of the bar is used to represent the frequency.

EXAMPLE

The weights of 30 workers in a factory are shown in the table:

Weight (kg)	Frequency
$45 \le W < 55$	7
$55 \le W < 65$	13
$65 \le W < 75$	6
$75 \le W < 85$	4

- $45 \le W < 55$, etc. are called class intervals – notice they are all equal in width. This means the weights are between 45 and 55 kg. A weight of 55 kg would be in the next group.

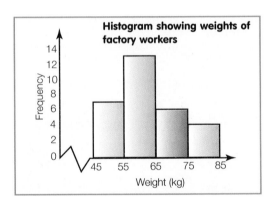

Histogram showing weights of factory workers

NOTE:
- The axes do not need to start at zero.
- The axes are labelled.
- The graph has a title.

REPRESENTING DATA

FREQUENCY POLYGONS

To draw a frequency polygon join the <u>midpoints of class intervals</u> for grouped or continuous data. Consider the histogram of the factory workers again.
- Put a cross on the middle of each bar and join the crosses up with a ruler.
- Draw a line down from the middle of the first and last bar to the x axis to form a closed polygon.
- To form an open polygon do not join to the x axis .

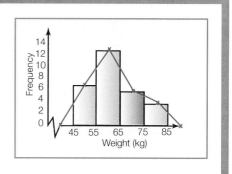

LINE GRAPHS

This example is known as a time series because the data is recorded at intervals of time

- These are a set of points joined by lines.

Year	1988	1989	1990	1991	1992	1993
Number of cars sold	2500	2900	2100	1900	1600	800

- <u>Middle</u> <u>values</u>, like point A, have no meaning. A does not mean that halfway between 1990 and 1991, there were 2000 cars sold.

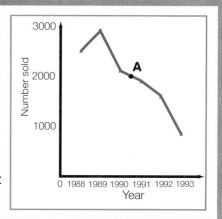

QUICK TEST

1. **For this set of data, draw a pie chart.**

Hair colour	Frequency
Brown	8
Auburn	4
Blonde	6
Black	6

2. **Using the histogram: a) complete the frequency table below.**

Height (cm)	Frequency
$140 \leq h < 145$	
$145 \leq h < 150$	10
$150 \leq h < 155$	
$155 \leq h < 160$	
$160 \leq h < 165$	

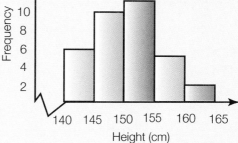

b) **How many people were in the survey?**

c) **Draw a frequency polygon on the histogram.**

TYPES OF CORRELATION

There are three types of correlation:

POSITIVE	NEGATIVE	ZERO

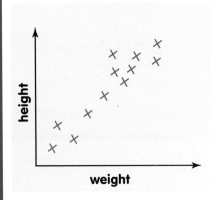

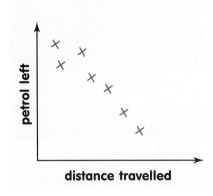

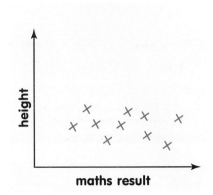

Positive
This is when both variables are increasing. If the points are nearly in a straight line there is said to be **high positive correlation**.

Negative
This is when one variable increases as the other decreases. If the points are nearly in a straight line there is said to be **high negative correlation**.

Zero
This is when there is little or no correlation between the variables.

DRAWING A SCATTER DIAGRAM

- Work out the scales first.
- Plot the points carefully.
- Each time a point is plotted, tick it off.

EXAMPLE

Maths test (%)	64	79	38	42	49	75	83	82	66	61	54
History test (%)	70	36	84	70	74	42	29	33	50	56	64

The table shows the Maths and History test results of 11 pupils.

The scatter diagram shows that there is a strong negative correlation – in general, the better the pupils did in Maths, the worse they did in History and vice versa.

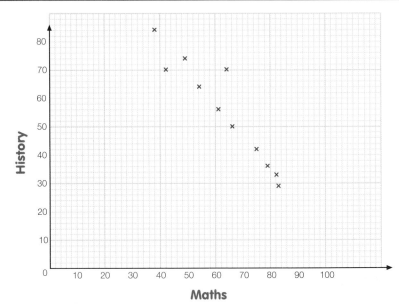

LINES OF BEST FIT

- **This is the line which best fits the data.** It goes in the direction of the data and has roughly the same number of points above the line as below it.
- A line of best fit can be used to make predictions.

EXAMPLE

If Hassam was away for a Maths test but got 78% in History then from the scatter diagram we can estimate he would have got approximately 44% in Maths.

⇨ Go to 78% on the History scale. Read across to the line then down.

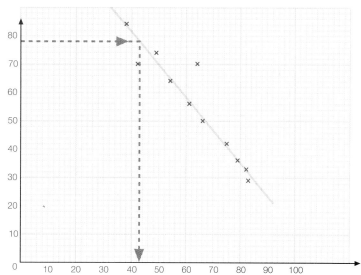

Scatter diagram showing Maths and History marks

SCATTER DIAGRAMS AND CORRELATION

- **A SCATTER DIAGRAM (SCATTER GRAPH OR SCATTER PLOT) IS USED TO SHOW TWO SETS OF DATA AT THE SAME TIME.**

- **ITS IMPORTANCE IS TO SHOW THE CORRELATION (CONNECTION) BETWEEN TWO SETS OF DATA.**

Examiner's Top Tip
Do not rush when drawing a scatter diagram. Plot the points very carefully. Remember to show on your graph how you made your estimates.

- -

QUICK TEST

For each pair of variables write down what type of correlation there is:

a) Number of pages in a magazine and the number of advertisements

b) The heights of students in a year group and the marks in the Maths test

c) The height up a mountain and the temperature

d) The age of a used car and its value

1. a) Positive b) Zero c) Negative d) Negative

AVERAGES 1

'Average height of students is 163 cm'

AVERAGES OF DISCRETE DATA

Do not round off

There are three types of average: mean, median and mode.

Mean: Sometimes known as the 'average'. Symbol for the mean is $\bar{x}$.

> **Mean = $\dfrac{\text{sum of a set of values}}{\text{the number of values used}}$**

Median: The middle value when the values are put in order of size.
Mode: The one that occurs the most often.
Range: This tells us how much the information is spread.
It is the highest value – lowest value.

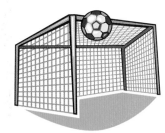

EXAMPLE

A football team scored the following number of goals in their first 10 matches:

2, 4, 0, 1, 2, 2, 3, 6, 2, 4

Find the mean, median, mode and range of the number of goals scored.

Mean = $\dfrac{2 + 4 + 0 + 1 + 2 + 2 + 3 + 6 + 2 + 4}{10}$ = $\dfrac{26}{10}$ = 2.6 goals

Median = 0, 1, 2, 2, 2, 2, 3, 4, 4, 6   Put in order of size

0̸ 1̸ 2̸ 2̸ ②② 3̸ 4̸ 4̸ 6̸ Cross off from the ends to find the middle.

$\dfrac{2 + 2}{2}$ = 2 goals

> If there are 2 numbers in the middle the median is halfway between them.

Mode = 2 goals because it occurs 4 times.

Range = 6 – 0 = 6

FINDING A MISSING VALUE WHEN GIVEN THE MEAN

If you are given the mean of a set of discrete data you can use the information to calculate a missing value.

EXAMPLE
The mean of 15, 17, y, 28 and 19 is 16. What is the value of y?

mean = $\dfrac{15 + 17 + y + 28 + 19}{5}$

$16 = \dfrac{79 + y}{5}$

so $16 \times 5 = 79 + y$

$80 = 79 + y$

so $y = 80 - 79$

$\underline{y = 1}$

> This just becomes a simple equation to solve.

FINDING AVERAGES FROM A FREQUENCY TABLE

• A frequency table tells us how many are in a group.

EXAMPLE

Number of sisters (x)	0	1	2	3	4
Frequency (f)	4	9	3	5	2

This means 2 people had 4 sisters.

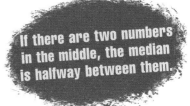

If there are two numbers in the middle, the median is halfway between them.

$\underline{\text{Mean}}\ (\bar{x}) = \dfrac{\Sigma f x}{\Sigma f}$

$= \dfrac{(4 \times 0) + (9 \times 1) + (3 \times 2) + (5 \times 3) + (2 \times 4)}{4 + 9 + 3 + 5 + 2 + 0}$

$= \dfrac{38}{23} = 1.7$ (to 1 d.p.)

Median Since there are 23 people who have been asked the median will be the 12th person.

    11 people   12   11 people

The 12th person has 1 sister ∴ the median = 1

Mode   This is the one with the highest frequency, that is 1 sister.

Range 4 − 0 = 4

Σ means the sum of

Remember this tip

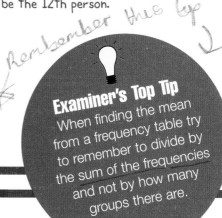

Examiner's Top Tip
When finding the mean from a frequency table try to remember to divide by the sum of the frequencies and not by how many groups there are.

MOVING AVERAGES

These are used to smooth out the changes in a set of data that varies over a period of time. A four-point moving average uses four data items in each calculation, a three point moving average uses three and so on.

A moving average can often give a good idea of any trend shown in a set of data as well as enabling you draw a trend line on a time series graph.

EXAMPLE
Find the three-point moving average for the following data.
2, 4, 0, 1, 2, 2, 3, 6, 2, 4.
Average for 1st 3 data points
Average for data points (2 → 4)

$(2 + 4 + 0) \div 3 = 2$
$(4 + 0 + 1) \div 3 = 1.\dot{6}$
$(0 + 1 + 2) \div 3 = 1$
$(1 + 2 + 2) \div 3 = 1.\dot{6}$
$(2 + 2 + 3) \div 3 = 2.\dot{3}$
$(2 + 3 + 6) \div 3 = 3.\dot{6}$
$(3 + 6 + 2) \div 3 = 3.\dot{6}$
$(6 + 2 + 4) \div 3 = 4$

QUICK TEST

1. Find the mean, median, mode and range of this set of data: 2, 9, 3, 6, 4, 4, 5, 8, 4

2. Charlotte made this table for the number of minutes students were late for registration

Number of minutes late (x)	0	1	2	3	4
Frequency (f)	10	4	6	3	2

Calculate:

a) the mean   b) the median   c) the mode   d) the range

1. mean = 5; median = 4; mode = 4; range = 7   2. a) mean = 1.32 mins b) median = 1 c) mode = 0 d) range = 4

TYPICAL GCSE QUESTION

Finding the mean of grouped data is a very common GCSE question and is usually worth about 4 marks.

EXAMPLE
The weight of some Year 9 pupils is shown below:

Weight (kg)	Frequency (f)	Midpoint (x)	fx
$40 \leqslant W < 45$	7	42.5	297.5
$45 \leqslant W < 50$	4	47.5	190
$50 \leqslant W < 55$	3	52.5	157.5
$55 \leqslant W < 60$	1	57.5	57.5

Adding on these columns helps show your working out.

This is the same as on page 81 except the frequency is multiplied by the <u>midpoint</u>.

<u>Mean</u> $= \dfrac{\Sigma fx}{\Sigma f} = \dfrac{(7 \times 42.5) + (4 \times 47.5) + (3 \times 52.5) + (1 \times 57.5)}{7 + 4 + 3 + 1}$

$= \dfrac{702.5}{15} = 46.8$ kg (1 d.p.)

<u>Modal class</u> $= 40 \leqslant W < 45$

Examiner's Top Tip
If your calculator will do statistic
learn how to use it. It is much
quicker but always do it twice
a check. Always try and sho
full working out in order to
obtain some method
marks.

STEM AND LEAF DIAGRAMS

Stem and leaf diagrams are another way of recording information and they can be used to find the mode, median and range of a set of data.

EXAMPLE
Here are some marks gained by some students in a mathematics exam.

24 61 55 36 42
32 60 51 38 58
55 52 47 55 55

When the information is put into a stem and leaf diagram it looks like this:

Stem is 30 leaf is 2 ∴ 32

stem	leaf
2	4
3	② 6 8
4	2 7
5	1 2 5 5 5 5 8
6	0 1

Stem = 10 marks

To read off the values you multiply the stem by 10 and add on the leaf. Using the stem and leaf, the mode, median and range can be found easily:

mode = 55
median = 52
range = 61 – 24
= 37

Stem and leaf diagrams are useful when comparing two sets of data.

USING AVERAGES AND SPREAD TO COMPARE DISTRIBUTIONS

Be careful when drawing conclusions from averages as they do not always tell the whole story.

EXAMPLE
11A obtained a mean of 57% in a test and the range was 79.
11T obtained a mean of 84% in the same test and the range was 18.

From the averages we would say that 11T is better than 11A. However if the range is looked at for each class:

11A = 100% – 21% = 79%
11T = 94% – 76% = 18%

Using the range it can be seen that not all of 11T are better than 11A, because some of 11A obtained higher marks than 11T.
The average of 11A has been lowered because of the low marks obtained by some pupils.

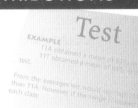

AVERAGES OF GROUPED DATA

- When the data are grouped into class intervals, the exact data are not known.
- Estimate the mean by using the <u>midpoint</u> of the <u>class</u> <u>interval</u>.
- The midpoint is the halfway value.
- When using grouped (continuous) data only the <u>modal</u> <u>class</u> can be found.
  This is the one with the highest frequency.

AVERAGES ②

USING APPROPRIATE AVERAGES

- The <u>mean</u> is useful when a 'typical' value is wanted.
  Be careful not to use the mean if there are extreme values.
- The <u>median</u> is a useful average to use if there are extreme values.
- The <u>mode</u> is useful when the most common value is needed.

QUICK TEST

1. The heights of some Year 10 pupils are shown in the table:

Height	Frequency
$140 \leq h < 145$	4
$145 \leq h < 150$	7
$150 \leq h < 155$	14
$155 \leq h < 160$	5
$160 \leq h < 165$	2

a) Calculate an estimate for the mean of this data.

b) Write down the modal class.

TYPICAL GCSE QUESTION

Ahmed carried out a survey for his Geography coursework. He recorded the distance that 200 people travelled to an out-of-town shopping centre. The table shows his findings.

Distance (d miles)	Frequency	Distance (d miles)	Cumulative Frequency
$0 \leq d < 5$	12	$0 \leq d < 5$	12
$5 \leq d < 10$	49	$0 \leq d < 10$	61
$10 \leq d < 15$	57	$0 \leq d < 15$	118
$15 \leq d < 20$	45	$0 \leq d < 20$	163
$20 \leq d < 25$	34	$0 \leq d < 25$	197
$25 \leq d < 30$	3	$0 \leq d < 30$	200

- To complete the cumulative frequency table the frequencies need to be added, e.g. 12 + 49 = 61.
- To check the cumulative frequency table is correct, the final value in the cumulative frequency column should be the same as the number of people in the survey.
- Plot (5, 12), (10, 61), etc. The **upper class** boundaries are used.
- Since no people had less than zero distance, the graph starts at (0, 0).
- Join the points with a smooth curve.

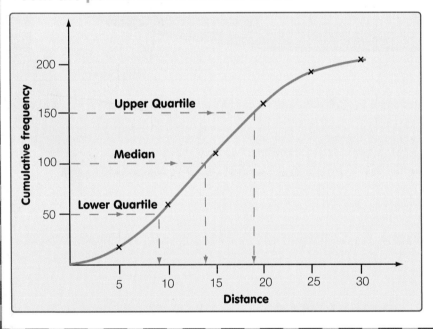

Examiner's Top Tip
Cumulative frequency graphs are one of the most common topics tested on the GCSE Intermediate/Higher level examination. Remember to:
- Draw graphs as accurately as possible. Try to avoid bumpy curves
- Check your graph looks like an S shape.
- Plot the upper class boundaries
- Show the method lines for the median, etc. on your graphs.

BOX AND WHISKER DIAGRAMS

All cumulative frequency graphs tend to have the same basic shape so they are not easy to compare.

A box and whisker diagram shows the interquartile range as a box, this then makes it useful when comparing distributions.

The box and whisker diagram for the cumulative frequency graph above would look like this:

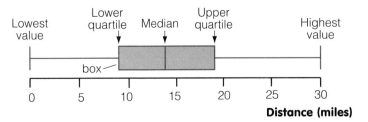

FINDING THE INTERQUARTILE RANGE

The interquartile range is found by subtracting the lower quartile from the upper quartile.

- Interquartile range = upper quartile – lower quartile
- Upper quartile This is the value three quarters of the way into the distribution.
  So $\frac{3}{4}$ x 200 = 150 approx. 18.7 miles for our data.
- Lower quartile This is the value one quarter of the way into the distribution.
  So $\frac{1}{4}$ x 200 = 50 approx. 9 miles for our data.
  The interquartile range for our data is 18.7 – 9 = 9.7 miles.

FINDING THE MEDIAN

The median is the middle value of the distribution.
For the distance data:
Median = $\frac{1}{2}$ x total cumulative frequency = $\frac{1}{2}$ x 200 = 100

- Reading across from 100 to the graph and then down
  gives a median distance of about 13.4 miles.

CUMULATIVE FREQUENCY GRAPHS

These are very useful for finding the median and the spread of grouped data.

USING THE INTERQUARTILE RANGE

A large interquartile range indicates that the 'middle half' of the data is widely spread about the median.

A small interquartile range indicates that the 'middle half' the data is concentrated about the median.

QUICK TEST

On another day Bethany also carried out the same survey. Her results are as follows:

Distance (d miles)	Frequency
0 ≤ d < 5	15
5 ≤ d < 10	60
10 ≤ d < 15	67
15 ≤ d < 20	30
20 ≤ d < 25	22
25 ≤ d < 30	6

1. Draw a cumulative frequency graph on the grid opposite.
2. Work out:
   a) the median
   b) interquartile range for this data.

2.a) Median approx. 12 miles
b) interquartile range = 9 miles (approx)

WHAT IS PROBABILITY?

<u>Exhaustive</u> <u>events</u> account for all possible outcomes.
For example, the list HH, HT, TH, TT gives all possible outcomes
when two coins are tossed simultaneously.
<u>Mutually</u> <u>exclusive</u> events are events that cannot happen at the same time.
For example if two students are chosen at random:

Event A: one student has brown hair
These are <u>not</u> <u>mutually</u> <u>exclusive</u> because brown-haired students can wear glasses.

Event B: one student wears glasses

Probability of an event = $\dfrac{\text{number of ways an event can happen}}{\text{total number of outcomes}}$

P(event) is a shortened way of writing probability of an event.

EXAMPLE
There are 6 blue, 4 yellow and 2 red beads in a bag.
John chooses a bead at random. What is the probability he chooses:

a) a red bead?
b) a yellow bead?
c) a blue, yellow or red bead?
d) a white bead?

a) P(red) = $\frac{2}{12}$ or $\frac{1}{6}$
b) P(yellow) = $\frac{4}{12}$ or $\frac{1}{3}$
c) P(blue, yellow or red) = $\frac{12}{12}$ = 1
d) P(white) = 0

PROBABILITY OF AN EVENT NOT HAPPENING

If two events are <u>mutually exclusive</u>, then
P(event will happen) = 1 − P (event will not happen)
or
P(event will not happen) = 1 − P (event will happen)

EXAMPLE
The probability that someone gets flu next winter is 0.42. What is the probability that they do not get flu next winter?
P(not get flu) = 1 − P (get flu)
= 1 − 0.42
= 0.58

EXPECTED NUMBER

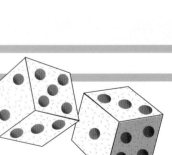

EXAMPLE
If a fair die is thrown 300 times, approximately how many fives are likely to be obtained?
P(5) = $\frac{1}{6}$ × 300 = 50 fives
We multiply 300 by $\frac{1}{6}$ since a 5 is expected $\frac{1}{6}$ of the time.

EXAMPLE
The probability of passing a driving test at the first attempt is 0.65. If there are 200 people taking their test for the first time, how many do you expect to pass the test?
0.65 × 200 = 130 people

RELATIVE FREQUENCIES

Relative frequencies can be used as an estimate of probability.
If it is not possible to calculate probability, an experiment is used to find the relative frequency.

Relative frequency of an event = $\dfrac{\text{number of times event occurred}}{\text{total number of trials}}$

EXAMPLE

When a fair die was thrown 80 times a six came up 12 times.
What is the relative frequency of getting a six?

number of trials = 80   relative frequency = $\dfrac{12}{80}$ = 0.15
number of sixes = 12

Examiner's Top Tip
Probabilities must be written as a fraction, decimal or percentage. Probabilities can never be greater than one.

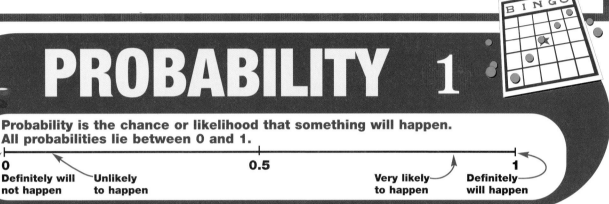

PROBABILITY 1

**Probability is the chance or likelihood that something will happen.
All probabilities lie between 0 and 1.**

0		0.5		1
Definitely will not happen	Unlikely to happen		Very likely to happen	Definitely will happen

USING EXPERIMENTS TO CALCULATE RELATIVE FREQUENCIES

If a die is thrown 180 times it would be expected that 30 twos would be thrown.
$\frac{1}{6}$ x 180 = 30

EXAMPLE

Throw the die 180 times but record the frequency of twos every 30 throws.

Number of throws	Total frequency of twos	Relative frequency
30	3	0.1
60	7	0.12
90	16	0.18
120	19	0.16
150	24	0.16
180	31	0.17

This value is obtained by dividing the total frequency of twos by number of throws, i.e. $\frac{16}{90}$.

- it is expected that $\frac{1}{6}$ = 0.16̇6̇ = 0.17 of the throws will be twos.
- as the number of throws increases, the relative frequency gets closer to the expected probability.

QUICK TEST

1. Write down an event that will have a probability of zero.

2. A box contains 3 salt 'n' vinegar, 4 cheese and 2 bacon flavoured packets
   of crisps. If a packet of crisps is chosen at random what is the probability that it is:
   a) salt 'n' vinegar?   b) cheese?   c) onion flavoured?

3. The probability that it will not rain tomorrow is $\frac{2}{9}$. What is the probability that it will rain tomorrow?

4. The probability of achieving a grade C in Mathematics is 0.48. If 500 students sit the exam
   how many would you expect to achieve a grade C?

5. When a fair die was thrown 200 times, a five came up 47 times. What is the relative
   frequency of getting a five?

1. Answers could be: I will get a 7 when I throw a die; or I will get a 4 when I throw a coin   2. a) $\frac{3}{9} = \frac{1}{3}$ b) $\frac{4}{9}$ c) 0   3. $\frac{7}{9}$
4. 240   5. $\frac{47}{200}$

THE MULTIPLICATION LAW

- When two events are <u>independent</u> the outcome of the second event is not affected by the outcome of the first.
- If two or more events are <u>independent</u>, the probability of A and B and C . . . happening together is found by <u>multiplying</u> the separate probabilities.

P(A and B and C . . .) = P(A) x P(B) x P(C) . . .

EXAMPLE
The probability that it will rain on any day in August is $\frac{3}{10}$. Find the probability that:
a) it will rain on both 1 August and 3 August.
b) it will rain on 9 August but not 20 August.

a) P (rain and rain) = $\frac{3}{10}$ x $\frac{3}{10}$ = $\frac{9}{100}$

b) P (rain and not rain) = $\frac{3}{10}$ x $\frac{7}{10}$ = $\frac{21}{100}$

THE ADDITION LAW

If two or more events are <u>mutually exclusive</u> the probability of A or B or C . . . happening is found by <u>adding</u> the probabilities.
P (A or B or C. . .)
= P(A) + P(B) + P(C) + . . .

EXAMPLE
There are 11 counters in a bag: 5 of the counters are red and 3 of them are white. Lucy picks a counter at random. Find the probability that Lucy's counter is either red or white.

P(red) = $\frac{5}{11}$ P(white) = $\frac{3}{11}$

P(red or white) = P(red) + P(white)

$\frac{5}{11} + \frac{3}{11} = \frac{8}{11}$ Red and white are mutually exclusive

Examiner's Top Tip
When answering questions that involve tree diagrams remember to:
- make sure that on each pair of branches the probabilities add up to 1
- multiply along the branches
- add the probabilities of there being more than one alternative, i.e. P(A or B).

TREE DIAGRAMS

These are another way of showing the possible outcomes of two or more events. They may be written horizontally or vertically.

EXAMPLE
In a class, the probability that a pupil will have his/her own television is $\frac{5}{7}$ and the probability that the pupil will have his/her own computer is $\frac{1}{4}$. These two events are independent.
Draw a tree diagram of this information.
- Draw the first branch which shows the probabilities of having televisions.
- Put the probabilities on the branches.
- Draw the second branches which show the probabilities of having computers.

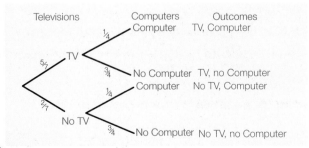

The multiplication and addition laws are useful when answering questions about tree diagrams.

a) Find the probability that a pupil will have their own TV and a computer.
P(TV and computer)   = P(TV) x P(computer)
= $\frac{5}{7}$ x $\frac{1}{4}$
= $\frac{5}{28}$

b) Find the probability that a pupil will have only one of the items.
P(TV and no computer) = P(TV) x P(no computer)
= $\frac{5}{7}$ x $\frac{3}{4}$
= $\frac{15}{28}$
OR
P(no TV and computer) = P(no TV) x P(computer)
= $\frac{2}{7}$ x $\frac{1}{4}$
= $\frac{2}{28}$

P(only one of the items)= $\frac{15}{28} + \frac{2}{28} = \frac{17}{28}$

SAMPLE SPACE DIAGRAMS

A table is helpful when considering outcomes of two events.
This kind of table is sometimes known as a <u>sample</u> <u>space</u> <u>diagram</u>.

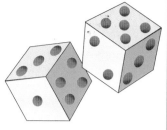

EXAMPLE

Two dice are thrown together and their scores are added. Draw a diagram to show all
the outcomes. Find the probability of:

a) a score of 7.

b) a score that is a multiple of 4.

a) P(score of 7) = $\frac{6}{36}$ = $\frac{1}{6}$

b) P(multiple of 4) = $\frac{9}{36}$ = $\frac{1}{4}$

		First die				
	1	**2**	**3**	**4**	**5**	**6**
1	2	3	④	5	6	⑦
2	3	④	5	6	⑦	⑧
Second **3**	④	5	6	⑦	⑧	9
die **4**	5	6	⑦	⑧	9	10
5	6	⑦	⑧	9	10	11
6	⑦	⑧	9	10	11	12

There are 36
outcomes.

PROBABILITY ②

QUICK TEST

1. The probability that Meena does her homework is 0.8. The probability that Fiona does her
homework is 0.45. Find the probability that both girls do their homework.

2. a) Draw a sample space diagram which shows the outcomes when two dice are thrown
together and their scores are multiplied.   b) What is the probability of a score of 6?
c) What is the probability of a score of 37?

3. A bag contains 3 red and 4 blue counters. If a counter is taken out of the bag at random,
its colour noted and then it is replaced, and a second counter is taken out, what is the
probability of choosing a counter of either colour? (Hint: use a tree diagram to help you.)

Die 1						
	1	**2**	**3**	**4**	**5**	**6**
1	1	2	3	4	5	6
2	2	4	6	8	10	12
3	3	6	9	12	15	18
4	4	8	12	16	20	24
5	5	10	15	20	25	30
6	6	12	18	24	30	36

Die 2

1. 0.36
2. a)
b) $\frac{2}{36}$ = $\frac{1}{18}$ c) 0   3. $\frac{24}{49}$

HANDLING DATA

1. The number of mm of rainfall that fell during the first eight days of August are shown below:
   a) Draw a line graph to display this information
   b) Work out the mean monthly rainfall for the first eight days of August.

Day	1	2	3	4	5	6	7	8
Rainfall	12	4	7	2	5	1	2	6

....

2. Reece carried out a survey to find out the favourite flavours of crisps of students in his class. The results are shown in the table (right). Draw a pie chart of this information.

Crisp flavour	Number of students
Cheese and onion	7
Salt and vinegar	10
Beef	6
Smokey bacon	1

3. Find the mean, median and mode of these quantities: 6, 2, 1, 4, 2, 2, 5, 3

   1, 2, 2, 2, 3, 4, 5, 6 = 25 = 3⅛ = mean   mode = 2

4. A bag contains three red, four blue and six green balls. If a ball is chosen at random from the bag, what is the probability of choosing:
   a) a red ball 3/13   b) a green ball 6/13   c) a yellow ball 0/13   d) a blue or red ball 7/13

....

5. The probability that Josie gets full marks on a tables test is 0.82. What is the probability that she does not get full marks on the tables test?

....

6. A youth club has 75 members. 42 of the members are boys.
   There are 15 members who are boys under 13 years old.
   There are 21 members who are girls over 13 years old.
   a) Complete the two-way table.
   b) How many girls are under 13 years old?

	Under 13 years old	13 years old and over	Totals
Boys			
Girls			
Total			

....

7. The pie chart below shows how Erin spends a typical day.
   a) Measure the size of the angle for sleeping ....
   b) Work out the number of hours that Erin works ....
   c) For how many hours does Erin watch TV?...

   Eating 30°
   Watching TV | Sleeping
   Working 120°

8. The probability of passing a driving test is 0.7.
   If 200 people take the driving test today, how many would you expect to pass?

....

9. Michelle is a swimmer. The probability of her winning a race is 84%. If she swims in 50 races this season, how many races would you expect her to win?

....

(C) 10. A die is thrown and the scores are noted.
   The results are shown in this table:
   Work out the mean die score.

Die score	1	2	3	4	5	6
Frequency	12	15	10	8	14	13

....

11. In a survey the heights of ten girls and their shoe sizes were measured:

Height in cm	150	157	159	161	158	164	154	152	162	168
Shoe size	3	5	5½	6	5	6½	4	3½	6	7

a) Draw a scatter diagram to illustrate this data:

 Indicates that a calculator may be used

b) What type of correlation is there between height and shoe size?......................................
c) Draw a line of best fit on your diagram ....
d) From your scatter diagram, estimate the height of a girl whose shoe size is $4\frac{1}{2}$. ....

12. Two spinners are used in a game. The first spinner is labelled 2, 4, 6, 8.
    The second spinner is labelled 3, 5, 5, 7. Both spinners are spun.
    The score is found by multiplying the numbers on each spinner.
a) Complete the table to show the possible scores:
b) What is the probability of getting an even score? ....
c) What is the probability of getting a score of 10? ....

		First spinner			
		2	4	6	8
Second spinner	3				
	5				
	5				
	7				

13. The weights of some students in a class are measured.
    These are the results:
a) Work out an estimate for the mean weight of the students.

....

b) What is the modal class? ....

Weight in kg	Number of students
$40 \le W < 45$	6
$45 \le W < 50$	5
$50 \le W < 55$	8
$55 \le W < 60$	4
$60 \le W < 65$	2

14. Ahmed and Matthew are going to take a swimming test.
    The probability that Ahmed will pass the swimming test is 0.85.
    The probability that Matthew will pass the swimming test is 0.6. The two events are independent.
a) Complete the probability tree diagram.

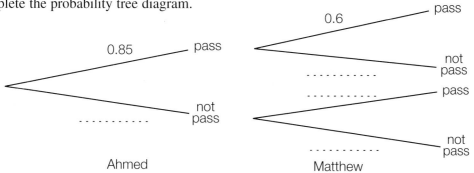

b) Work out the probability that both Ahmed and Matthew
   will pass the swimming test ....
c) Work out the probability that one of them will pass the swimming test
   and the other will not pass the swimming test ....

15. The table shows the time in minutes
    for 83 peoples' journeys to work.
a) Complete the cumulative frequency
   column in the table.
b) Draw a cumulative frequency graph of the data.
c) From your graph find the median.

....

Time in minutes	Frequency	Cumulative frequency
$0 \le t < 10$	5	
$10 \le t < 20$	20	
$20 \le t < 30$	26	
$30 \le t < 40$	18	
$40 \le t < 50$	10	
$50 \le t < 60$	4	

d) From your graph find the interquartile range ....
e) How many people had a journey of more than 45 minutes to work?.......................................

How did you do?

1–5	correct	....start again
6–10	correct	....getting there
11–12	correct	....good work
13–15	correct	....excellent

EXAM QUESTIONS - Use the questions to test your progress. Check your answers on page 95.

1. Audrey paid £3.12 for 13 pencils. Each pencil cost the same. Work out the cost of each pencil.

....

2. Write these numbers in order of size, start with the smallest number: 0.6, 65%, $\frac{1}{2}$, $\frac{6}{7}$, $\frac{3}{8}$

....

3. Rashid carried out a survey to find out the favourite subjects of 24 students. Draw a pie chart of this data.

Subject	Frequency
Maths	9
English	4
Art	6
German	5

4. Draw a plane of symmetry on this shape:

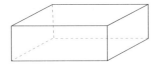

(C) 5. Jonathan is buying a new television. He sees three different advertisements for the same television set. Work out the cost of the televisions in each advertisement.

a)

Ed's Electrical Goods

TVs Normal Price
£250

Sale: 10% off

b)

Sheila's Bargains

TVs £185
+ VAT at 17½%

c)

GITA'S TV SHOP

Normal Price
£290

SALE: $\frac{1}{5}$ Off
Normal Price

6. A box of crisps contains 50 packets of different flavoured crisps. There are four flavours: cheese, bacon, beef and tomato, in each box. The probability of each flavour in each box is:

Flavour	Cheese	Bacon	Beef	Tomato
Probability	0.3	0.1	X	0.45

a) Calculate the value of X.
b) Write down the most common flavour of crisp. ....
c) If a packet of crisps is taken out of the box at random
   what is the probability that it is either cheese or bacon flavoured? ....
d) For a party Mary buys six boxes of crisps. Estimate how many
   packets of crisps will be tomato flavoured. ....

7. Solve the following equations:
a) $2X - 4 = 10$ ....
b) $6X - 3 = 4X + 9$ ....
c) $5(2X + 1) = 20$ ....

8. On the grid below, draw the image of the shaded shape after:
   a) A reflection in the line $y = X$. Call the image B.
   b) A rotation of 180° about the origin (0, 0). Call the image C.
   c) A translation by the vector $\binom{-5}{4}$. Call the image D.

(C) 9. A circle has a radius of 36 cm. Work out the circumference of the circle. Give your answer correct to the nearest cm

....

(C) 10. $s = ut + \frac{1}{2}at^2$. Calculate the value of s when $u = -6$, $t = 4.2$ and $a = \frac{5}{8}$.

....

(C) 11. The diagram shows a triangular prism. Work out the volume of the prism, clearly stating your units. Give your answer to three s.f.

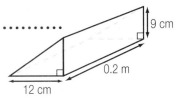

9 cm

0.2 m

12 cm

....

(C) Indicates that a calculator may be used

12. Saimia ran the 100 metre race in a time of 14.3 seconds to the nearest tenth of a second. What is the shortest time that she ran the race in?

....

13. Calculate the length of the diagonal of this rectangle, giving your answer to 1 decimal place.

22.3 cm

9.2 cm

....

14. £360 is invested for 3 years at 5% compound interest, which is paid annually. What is the total interest earned?

....

15. Using a trial and improvement method or otherwise solve the equation $t^3 - t = 15$. Show full working out and give your answer to one decimal place.

....

....

16. The mass of an atom is 2×10^{-23} grams. What is the total mass of 9×10^{15} of these atoms?

....

....

17. Matthew and Emily are going to take their driving tests. The probability that Matthew will pass the driving test is 0.75. The probability that Emily will pass the driving test is 0.8. The two events are independent.

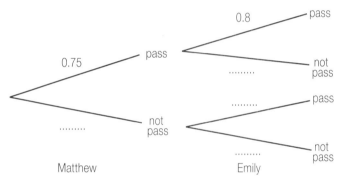

a) Complete the probability tree diagram.
b) Work out the probability that both Matthew and Emily
   will pass the driving test. ....
c) Work out the probability that one of them will pass the driving
   test and the other one will not pass the driving test. ....

18. ABCD is a quadrilateral. Angle DBA = 90°, Angle DBC = 40°, AB = 8 cm, BD = 6 cm.
a) Calculate the size of angle DAB. Give your answer correct to 3 s.f.

....

....

b) Calculate the length of DC. Give your answer correct to 3 s.f.

....

....

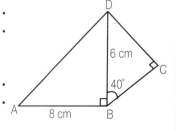

How did you do?

1–5	correct	....start again
6–10	correct	....getting there
11–15	correct	....good work
16–18	correct	....excellent

Number

1. a) 9, 21, 41 b) 9, 64, 100 c) 2, 41 d) 2, 40 e) 40, 64, 100

2. 9°

3. a) 44 764 b) 27

4. 8 boxes

5. 77.3%

6. £315

7. 750 g self raising flour, 375 g butter
   625 g sugar, 5 eggs

8. £25000

9. a) 365 b) 0.706

10. $\dfrac{9 + 9}{0.2 \times 50} = \dfrac{18}{10} = 1.8$

11. The 100 ml tube of toothpaste.

12. 1.5 cm

13. £376.47

14. £6502.50

15. £715.02

16. 20%

17. a) 2.67×10^6 b) 4.27×10^3
    c) 3.296×10^{-2} d) 2.7×10^{-2}

18. a) 4.2×10^{-5} g b) 2.52×10^1 g

19. a) 1.2×10^{22} b) 2×10^{11}

Algebra

1. $T = 85y + 8z$

2. a)
   b)

Pattern number	Number of matchsticks
1	4
2	7
3	10
4	13
5	16
6	19

c) 301 matchsticks   d) $m = 3p + 1$

3. a) $X = 3$ b) $X = 4$ c) $X = 5$ d) $X = 2$ e) $X = 1$

4. a) $9X + 4 = 22$ b) 3 cm is the shortest side

5. a)

X	−2	−1	0	1	2	3
$y = 3X - 4$	−10	−7	−4	−1	2	5

b) c) $(\frac{4}{3}, 0)$

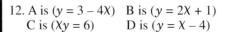

6. $2n^2 + 1$

7. a) $12X^4$ b) $12X^5 y^3$
   c) $4y^3$ d) $9y^4$

8. $a = 3$, $b = -2$

9. $P = 54.3$ (3 s.f.) b) $y = \dfrac{P^2 + 3X^2}{5X}$

10. $X = 1.8$

11. $1 \le n \le 3$

12. A is $(y = 3 - 4X)$ B is $(y = 2X + 1)$
    C is $(Xy = 6)$ D is $(y = X - 4)$

13. Graph 1 = C   Graph 2 = A   Graph 3 = B

14. a) $g(g + 10)$ b) $g(g + 10) = 11$, $g^2 + 10g = 11$
    c) Length = 11 : width = 1

Shape, Space and Measures

1. a) 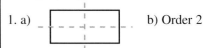 b) Order 2

2. $a = 80°$ $b = 50°$ $c = 130°$ $d = 15°$

3. a) 74
   b) 10.75

4. 1.32 lbs

5. 7.5 km

6.

7. a) 122.5m^2
   b) 63.6cm^2

8. 4 hr 55 min

9. 52.5 m.p.h.

10. 239.5 miles

11. 5.2 m

12. 1 940 000 cm^3

13. 9.2 m

14. 325° (nearest degree)

15. a) (i) XMN = 83°
       (ii) XNM = XZY = 68° Angles in a triangle add
       up to 180°, therefore 180° − 68° − 29° = 83°
    b) 3.65 cm
    c) 11.74 cm

16. l $\sqrt{r^2 + t^2}$; πr^2; 2tl

Handling Data

1. a)
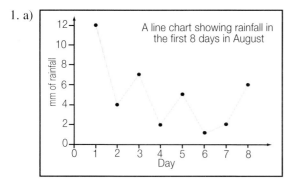

b) 4.875 mm

2.

Crisp flavour	No of students	Angle
Cheese & Onion	7	105°
Salt & Vinegar	10	150°
Beef	6	90°
Smokey Bacon	1	15°

3. mean = 3.125
    median = 2.5
    mode = 2

4. a) $\frac{3}{13}$ b) $\frac{6}{13}$ c) 0 d) $\frac{7}{13}$

5. 0.18

6. a)
b) 12 girls

	Under 13 yrs	13 yrs +	Totals
Boys	15	27	42
Girls	12	21	33
Total	27	48	75

7. a) 120°
b) 8 h
c) 6 h

8. 140 people

9. 42 races

10. 3.5

11. a)
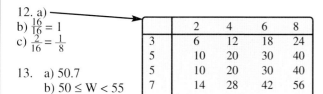

b) Positive correlation
c) See scatter diagram
d) 155.5 cm

12. a)
b) $\frac{16}{16} = 1$
c) $\frac{2}{16} = \frac{1}{8}$

	2	4	6	8
3	6	12	18	24
5	10	20	30	40
5	10	20	30	40
7	14	28	42	56

13. a) 50.7
     b) $50 \leq W < 55$

14. a) 0.51
     b) 0.43

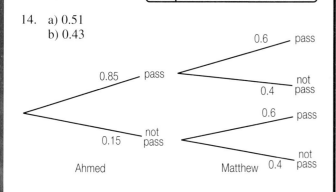

15. a)

Time (mins)	Frequency	Cumulative frequency
$0 \leq t < 10$	5	5
$10 \leq t < 20$	20	25
$20 \leq t < 30$	26	51
$30 \leq t < 40$	18	69
$40 \leq t < 50$	10	79
$50 \leq t < 60$	4	83

b)
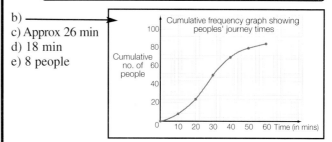

c) Approx 26 min
d) 18 min
e) 8 people

Mixed

1. 24p

2. $\frac{3}{8}$, $\frac{1}{2}$, 0.6, 65%, $\frac{6}{7}$

3. 3 possible planes as shown

4.
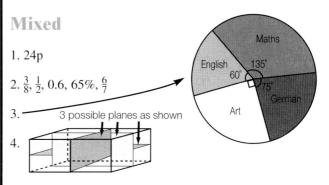

5. a) £225   b) £217.38   c) £232

6. a) 0.15   b) Tomato   c) 0.4   d) approx. 135

7. a) $X = 7$ b) $X = 6$ c) $X = \frac{3}{2}$ or 1.5

8.
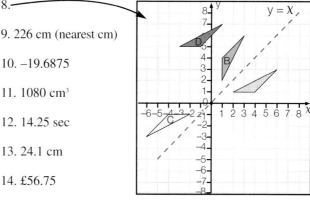

9. 226 cm (nearest cm)

10. −19.6875

11. 1080 cm³

12. 14.25 sec

13. 24.1 cm

14. £56.75

15. t = 2.6

16. 1.8×10^{-7} grams

17. a) See below
b) 0.6
c) 0.35

18. a) $36.87° = 36.9°$ (3 s. f.) b) 3.86

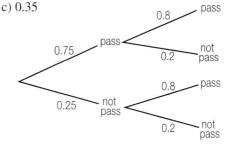
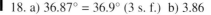